FAMOUS **BOMBER AIRCRAFT**

FAMOUS
BOMBER
AIRCRAFT

MARTIN W. BOWMAN

Patrick Stephens Limited

First published in 1989

British Library Cataloguing in Publication Data

Bowman, Martin W., 1952-
Famous bomber aircraft
1. Bomber aeroplanes
I. Title
623.74'63

ISBN 1-85260-094-2

Pictures not credited otherwise belong to the
author.

Patrick Stephens is part of the Thorsons
Publishing Group

Typeset by Burns & Smith, Derby

Printed in Great Britain by The Bath Press

10 9 8 7 6 5 4 3 2

CONTENTS

INTRODUCTION

Before reading this book try to imagine a selection of the most significant famous bombers since 1914, bearing in mind that the period since the First World War to the beginning of the Second must include around a dozen such types and a similar number of post-war designs must also feature. Difficult! When your list is compiled compare it with my personal selection contained herein.

While it is noticeable that predominately British bombers figure in the list of the First World War and between the wars bombers, notable exceptions are the Boeing B-9 and Martin B-10. American prominence in bomber design started with these two types and during the Second World War American industry delivered thousands upon thousands of B-17 Flying Fortresses, B-24 Liberators, B-25 Mitchells and B-29 Superfortresses. No book about famous bombers would be complete without the Avro Lancaster, the best bomber of the war, and the stalwart Vickers Armstrong Wellington.

Post-war British V-bombers are, of course, worthy of inclusion even though now the Victor and Valiant are perhaps first thought of in their role as tanker aircraft. Although it never reached RAF service, the superb TSR-2 is featured, many of its innovations being incorporated in other designs which followed. Although perhaps considered as reconnaissance aircraft the Soviet built Tupolev Tu-16 and Tu-20 were originally designed as long-range bombers. They also provide an opportunity to show to good advantage some of the superb photographs of these aircraft taken by intercepting NATO airmen.

Possibly all of the above will by now feature in nearly every personal list of famous bombers since 1914.

Martin W. Bowman

AIRCO (de HAVILLAND) DH 4

Type: *Light day bomber;* **Crew:** *Two;* **Manufacturers:** *Aircraft Manufacturing Co, Hendon. Subcontracted by FW Berwick & Co; Westland Aircraft and Vulcan Motor & Engineering Co;* **Powerplant:** *One RAF 3a or BHP or Rolls-Royce Eagle III/VI/VII/VIII;* **Dimensions:** *Span,42 ft 6 in (12.9 m); Length, 30 ft 3 in (9.2 m); Height, 10 ft 8 in (3.2 m);* **Weight:** *Loaded, 3,466 lb (1,572 kg);* **Performance:** *(With 360 hp Rolls-Royce Eagle) Max speed, 136 mph (218.87 km/h) at 6,500 ft (1,982 m) Ceiling, 23,000 ft (7,014 m)*

The DH 4 was among the first British aircraft designed for use as a light day bomber and was the finest of its type to see service in the First World War. Designed for reconnaissance and bombing, the DH 4 was a conventional and extremely strong aircraft, and its first flight in August 1916 and subsequent service trials proved highly successful.

The type first entered service with No 55 Squadron (RFC), which was sent to France fully-equipped on 6 March 1917. In April, the DH 4 was first used in action on a daylight bombing operation against railway sidings at Valenciennes. During March–April 1917, the DH 4 began equipping Nos 2 and 5 (Naval) Squadrons of the RNAS. No 2 Squadron operated the DH 4 on reconnaissance operations and in April 1918, this unit, now renumbered No. 202 Squadron, made an aerial reconnaissance of the entire defensive system at Ostend and Zeebrugge.

Because of engine shortages and the poor output produced by the original BHP engine in the prototype, many different powerplants were employed in the DH 4. The first production aircraft was fitted with a 250 hp Rolls-Royce Eagle engine replacing the BHP engines used by the prototypes. Eventually, the 375 hp Rolls-Royce Eagle VIII proved the most reliable

One of 150 Westland-built DH 4s. The first DH 4 to be produced at Yeovil was flight-tested in April 1917 by B. C. Hucks, a well-known aerobatic pilot, and was flown direct to France the morning after the initial test (Westland Aircraft).

of all powerplants used and gave the best performance.

From August 1917, DH 4s operated with the RNAS at Great Yarmouth, Norfolk, on Home Defence duties. On 5 August 1918, a DH 4 from this station flown by Major E. Cadbury and Captain R. Leckie, destroyed a Zeppelin. On the Western Front the DH 4 excelled in the day bombing role, carrying a bomb load of up to 460 lb (208.7 kg) on racks beneath the fuselage and wings. Some DH 4s were supplied to Belgium and although it was intended in 1917 to supply 50 260 hp Fiat-engined DH 4s to Russia, none was ever sent there during that year and the aircraft concerned were taken over by the RFC.

By the end of 1918 American companies had built 4,587 DH 4s, of which 3,106 were manufactured by the Dayton-Wright Airplane Company of Ohio, while in Britain six companies turned out a total of only 1,449. The American-built versions were fitted with the 400 hp Liberty 12 or 435 hp Liberty 12A engine. After the war many of the British-built machines were refurbished for commercial use, although military versions remained in service with various air forces until as late as 1932.

AVRO LANCASTER

Type: *Heavy bomber*; **Crew:** *Seven*; **Manufacturers:** *A.V. Roe & Co Ltd, Manchester. Sub-contracted by Armstrong Whitworth, Austin, Metropolitan-Vickers and Vickers-Armstrong (Chester & Castle Bromwich);* **Powerplant:** *(I) Four Merlin 20/22/24;* **Dimensions:** *(I) Span, 102 ft (31.1 m); Length, 69 ft 4 in (21.1 m); Height, 19 ft 7 in (5.97 m);* **Weight:** *(I) Empty, 36,900 lb (16,705 kg); Loaded, 68,000 lb (30,800 kg);* **Performance:** *(I) Max speed, 287 mph (462 km/h) at 11,500 ft (3,500 m);* **Armament:** *(I) Two .303 machine-guns in nose, dorsal and ventral turrets, four .303 machine-guns in tail turret, 14,000 lb (6,350 kg) bomb load or one 22,000 lb bomb.*

The most successful and one of the most famous bombers in history began life in 1940 when a decision was taken to build a longer span version of the Manchester and re-engine it with four Rolls-Royce Merlins following the failure of the Vulture engine. On 9 January 1941, the first Lancaster flew as the Manchester III and was originally fitted with triple fins. Later that month it was flown to Boscombe Down for acceptance tests, and as a result the 33 ft (10.05 m) tailplane with twin fins and rudders was introduced and became standard on all production models.

Its designer, Roy Chadwick, had the foresight to allow from the outset, a bomb bay big enough to carry a bomb load of 4,000 lb (1,814 kg) and this was rapidly enlarged as the war progressed. On 13 May 1941, the second prototype Lancaster flew for the first time. It proved so successful that it went into immediate production after two months of trial installations at Woodford, and Manchesters already on the production line were completed

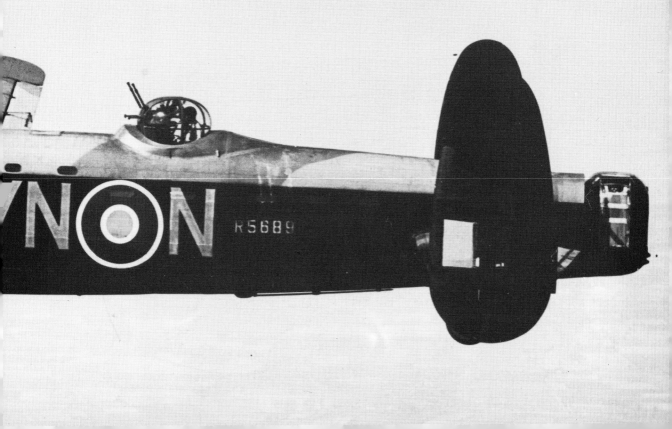

Avro Lancaster Mk I R5689 of No 50 Squadron in mid-1942 (via Mike Bailey).

as Lancasters. These were distinguishable from subsequent aircraft by their rectangular windows along the rear fuselage.

On 31 October 1941, the first production Lancaster I took to the air for the first time. It introduced a dorsal and ventral turret and four Merlin XX engines in place of earlier Merlin Xs used on the two prototypes. Deliveries began in early 1942 to No 44 Squadron at Waddington, followed by No 97 Squadron at Woodhall Spa. On 3 March 1942, four aircraft from No 44 Squadron flew the first Lancaster operation of the war with a mine-laying sortie in the Heligoland Bight. On the night of 10/11 March, two Lancasters from No 44 Squadron made the first Lancaster night operation with a raid on Essen. As if to prove how exceptional the Lancaster was, on 17 April 1942 12 aircraft from Nos 44 and 97 Squadrons, led by Squadron Leader J.D. Nettleton, carried out an ambitious low-level daylight attack on the MAN Diesel plant at Augsburg. Nettleton was awarded the Victoria Cross for his part in the raid.

On the night of 15/16 September 1943, two Lancasters of 617 Squadron (five of the eight despatched were lost) dropped the first 12,000 lb bombs, during the disastrous low-level raid on the Dortmund Ems canal. On 8 June 1944, the first deep penetration 12,000 lb Tallboy bombs were dropped by 19 Lancasters of No 617 Squadron on the tunnel at Saumur. The heaviest of all was the 22,000 lb 'Grand Slam', the first of which was dropped on the Bielefeld Viaduct on 14 March 1945 from a 617 Squadron Lancaster.

Altogether, Lancasters dropped 608,612 tons of bombs in 156,000 sorties. Among the most famous were those flown by No 617 squadron, especially created in 1943 under the command of Wing Commander Guy Gibson, primarily to destroy the Möhne, Eder and Sorpe dams in the Ruhr. The aircraft of what was to become legendary as the 'Dambusters' squadron, were equipped with a special dam-breaching weapon designed by Dr Barnes Wallis. This was a cylindrical missile that was rotated before release to emphasize its skipping progress across the surface of the water and subsequently to assist the weapon to roll downwards once it had made contact with the dam, thus ensuring that it quickly reached the depth at which its pressure-sensitive detonators caused it to explode. To hit their targets, Gibson and his crews had to fly in over the dam approaches at precisely 60 ft (18.2 m) above the water, each

aircraft being fitted with two spotlights arranged to coincide as a single spot of light when the aircraft was at exactly the right height.

For weeks 617 Squadron practised spinning their bombs on water in the Lake District until on the night of 16/17 May 1943 19 crews set out for the Ruhr. The Möhne and Eder dams were breached and some 330 million tons of water wrecked more than 100 factories in the Ruhr. A heavy, low mist shielded the Sorpe Dam making accurate bombing impossible. The operation cost eight Lancasters and their crews. Gibson was awarded the Victoria Cross for his leadership on the raid and for drawing enemy fire on his own aircraft.

Lancasters flew many other famous raids and as early as July 1943 they had proved the best Allied bomber in Europe, dropping 132 tons of bombs for every Lancaster lost on operations. This compared with only 56 tons (later 86) for the Halifax and 41 for the Stirling. The Lancaster could not fly as high as its American contemporaries, but it could haul a 14,000 lb (6,350 kg) bomb load almost as far as the B-24 and much further than the Halifax. The B-17 and B-24 could only carry a typical load of 4,000 lb (1,818 kg) and 5,000 lb (2,272 kg) respectively.

During 1944, Lancasters flew daylight tactical missions in support of the invasion forces around Caen in the days immediately following D-Day. On 12 November 1944, 18 Lancasters from 617 Squadron and 13 from No 9 Squadron dropped 12,000 lb bombs to capsize the German battleship *Tirpitz* in a Norwegian fiord. Other famous epic raids occurred with the Pathfinder Force, which first began operations in August 1942 and continued throughout the war marking the targets for succeeding waves of Lancasters and other bombers. The tenth and final VC awarded to a Lancaster crewmember went to Captain E. Swales, South African Air Force, who was master-bomber of a force that bombed Pforzheim on 23 February 1945. Swales remained at the controls until his crew had baled out of the doomed Lancaster but he was found dead after the aircraft crashed. Group Captain Leonard Cheshire was awarded the VC, while Commanding Officer of 617 Squadron after completing 100 operations, many of them in Lancasters.

By March 1945, Bomber Command boasted no fewer than 56 squadrons of 'Lancs' on first-line duty (745 operational Lancasters and 296 more in OTUs). On 25 April 1945, Lancasters symbolically flew their last daylight operation

Left *Lancaster B Mk I of 463 (Canadian) Squadron* (Ashley Annis).

Right *Lancaster B Mk I NG347 QB-P Piccadily Princess of No 424 (Canadian) Squadron, built by Armstrong Whitworth* (Ashley Annis).

Above *Lancaster I (FE)s of No 35 (Madras Presidency) Squadron en route to their goodwill tour of the USA in 1946 (Ashley Annis).*

Left *Lancaster B Mk VII WU15 (formerly NX611) of the French L'Aeronavale at Changi in 1965 during a flight from Australia to the UK where, after flying briefly in 1967-68, it was finally grounded and became the gate guardian at RAF Scampton, Lincs (Jerry Cullum).*

of the war with a raid on Hitler's mountain retreat at Berchtesgaden. On the night of 25/26 April, Lancasters made the final night raid of the war with an attack on an oil target at Vallo, Norway.

Altogether, 7,377 Lancasters were built, including 430 in Canada by Victory Aircraft. The main production variants were the Mk I (3,425 built) and the Mk III (3,039 built with Packard-Merlin engines). Some Mk I (Special) variants were built to accommodate 8,000 lb (3,633 kg), 12,000 lb (5,443 kg) or 22,000 lb (9,979 kg) bomb loads. The Mk I (FE) was built to equip 'Tiger Force' for the proposed bombing of Japan. The last Lancaster to enter service was a Mk I (FE) in February 1946 and that same year Lancasters of No 35 Squadron made a goodwill tour of the USA.

During the immediate post-war period lend-lease Liberators were withdrawn from service and Lancasters operated with Coastal Command for a number of years until replaced by the Shackleton. Other variants served as photo-reconnaissance and ASR aircraft and the last Lancaster, a PR I, was retired from Bomber Command in December 1953. The last 'Lanc' in RAF service, an MR 3, was retired in February 1954 after service in Malta.

AVRO VULCAN

Type: *(BI/B 2) Long-range medium bomber;* **Crew:** *Five;* **Manufacturers:** *A.V. Roe & Co Ltd, Manchester;* **Powerplant:** *(B 2) Four Bristol Siddeley Olympus 201/301;* **Dimensions:** *Span, (B 2) 111 ft (33.83 m); Length, 105 ft 6 in (32.15 m); Height, 27 ft 2 in (8.26 m);* **Weight:** *(B 2) Loaded, 170,000 lb (77.272 kg);* **Performance:** *(B 2) Max speed, Mach 0.98 (645 mph (1038 km/h); Ceiling, 65,000 ft (19.810 m); Range, 4,600 miles (7,400 km);* **Armament:** *21 x 1,000 lb HE bombs or nuclear payload or Blue Steel 'stand-off' bomb.*

The Avro Vulcan was first bomber in the world to adopt the delta wing plan-form and the second V-bomber to enter RAF service. Built to specification B 35/46 issued in January 1947, the prototype flew for the first time on 30 August 1952. The second prototype differed from the first in having more powerful Bristol Olympus 101 engines in place of the 6,500 lb (2,954 kg) thrust Rolls-Royce Avons. This powerplant was fitted as standard to all the

Vulcan B 2A XL321 of No 617 Squadron carrying a Blue Steel stand off air-to-ground missile. The 'Dambusters' was the first operational Blue Steel squadron, in February 1963 (Hawker Siddeley).

Classic study of Vulcan B2 XL320 (BAe).

production Vulcans, the first of which made its maiden flight on 4 February 1955.

Despite its enormous size the Vulcan could demonstrate almost fighter-like manoeuvrability at very low altitudes. At the Farnborough Air Show in September 1955 test pilot Roly Falk caused a sensation by slow-rolling the aircraft during its flyby.

The Vulcan Mk I began equipping No 83 Squadron at Waddington on 21 May 1957, when four were received from No 230 OCU on temporary loan. The first of the Squadron's own aircraft arrived on 11 July 1957. Al-

together, 45 Mk Is were built and ultimately equipped eight squadrons. The B 1 could reach a height of about 55,000 ft (46,768 m) and fly at a maximum speed of about 620 mph (998.4 km/h). One of the most famous squadrons to operate the Vulcan was No 617, the 'Dambusters'. On 21 June 1961, a Vulcan IA from this squadron made the first non-stop flight from the UK to Australia, covering 11,500 miles (18,519 km) in just over 20 hours and being refuelled three times by Valiant tankers operating from Cyprus, Pakistan and Singapore.

The B 2, which entered service with No 83 Squadron at Waddington in July 1960, introduced a new, thinner wing of greater span and greater chord in the outboard sections. The B 2 was fitted with 17,000 lb (7,727 kg) thrust Olympus 200 series engines, later versions being fitted with the Olympus 300 engine of 22,000 lb (10,000 kg) thrust.

The B 2 had a service ceiling of about 65,000 ft (19,810 m) and a greater load carrying capability than the B 1. Most B 2s were equipped to carry a Blue Steel 'stand-off' missile. In 1962, No 617 Squadron became the first V-bomber squadron to become operational with the device. In 1964 it was announced that the force of about 50 would be switched to a low-level role. In 1966 Vulcans became operational in their new role, carrying up to 20 1,000 lb gravity bombs or a nuclear payload up to a maximum range of about 4,600 miles (7,400 km).

From 1973 to March 1982 No 27 Squadron used the SR 2 strategic reconnaissance version. From 1981 the Vulcan force was run down with the Tornado destined to replace the Vulcans in total. On 22 December 1981 No 617

Squadron disbanded, and five more Vulcan squadrons followed in 1982. Three remaining squadrons—Nos 44, 50 and 101—had been scheduled for disbandment on 30 June. However, the Falklands conflict broke out at the end of April 1982.

On 30 April/1 May two Vulcan B Mk 2s operating from Ascension Island, set off for the first bombing mission of the Falklands campaign. XM598 was forced to return, but XM607 completed the 16-hour mission (made possible by in-flight refuellings from Victor tankers) and bombed Port Stanley airfield. It was the first time a Vulcan had dropped bombs and fired missiles in anger in its 25-year history. Four more attacks, code-named 'Black Buck', were made against Argentinian targets, culminating on 12 June. On the 3 June mission, XM607 (which flew three of the five strikes) was forced to divert to Brazil after an in-flight refuelling incident involving the loss of its probe on the return leg of an anti-radar strike on the Falklands.

As a result of experience gained in the Falklands, six Vulcan K Mk 2 tankers were quickly organized to meet the urgent need for extra tanker capacity. By the end of 1982 all Vulcan bombers were retired. On 30 March 1984 No 50 Squadron disbanded, thus marking the end of the Vulcan in RAF service, although happily one has been retained for flying displays on the air show circuit.

BAC TSR-2

Type: *Tactical strike & reconnaissance;* **Crew:** *Two;* **Manufacturers:** *British Aircraft Corporation, Bristol;* **Powerplant:** *Two Bristol-Siddeley Olympus 22R Mk320 turbojets;* **Dimensions:** *Span, 37 ft (11.29 m); Length, 89 ft (27.18 m); Height, 24 ft (7.32 m);* **Weight:** *Empty, 95,900 lb (43,539 kg); Loaded, 105,000 lb (47,670 kg);* **Performance:** *Max speed, Mach 2.05 above 36,000 ft (10,980 m);* **Armament:** *Nuclear stores or three triple clutches of 1,000 lb.*

The TSR-2 was conceived in 1957 when the Air Staff issued a general operational require-

ment, called GOR 339, for a tactical strike and reconnaissance (TSR) aircraft to replace the Canberra. Its concept was revolutionary, embodying the latest advances in structures, propulsion, systems and materials, and associated

XR219, the only BAC TSR-2 to fly (Vickers).

costs. English Electric, under Mr. F. Page, and Vickers (Weybridge), under Mr. H.H. Gardner, began formulating designs.

Unfortunately for supporters of the TSR-2, government thinking was aimed at replacing all aircraft with the missile (as stated in the *Statement of Defence* which was prepared by Duncan Sandys in 1961). The British aircraft industry was also in upheaval. English Electric and Vickers' designs were subsequently merged with the formation of BAC. The two Olympus reheat turbojets were built by Bristol-Siddeley after Bristol and Hawker Siddeley were merged.

The TSR-2 was without question the most highly-advanced aircraft of its time, possibly too advanced for its own good. Variable sweep wings were considered as a means of obtaining the required STOL performance, but this was rejected in favour of a very broad fixed wing with powerful blown flaps across the entire span, except for the down-turned tips. A flight control system far in advance of any other in the world at that time drove these surfaces and could carry out any manoeuvres generated by the pilot, terrain-following radar or by the weapon delivery system. The TSR-2 was also the first British aircraft fitted with an in-flight refuelling probe.

On 7 October 1960, the main development contract for the TSR-2 was signed and there were hopes that the RAAF would also buy the aircraft. However, in 1963 the Australians bought the American F-111, a decision made in part because it was stated by the British Labour Party that if elected at the next General Election, it would cancel the TSR-2 programme.

The first production TSR-2 made its maiden flight on 27 September 1964, but six months later Harold Wilson's Government axed the programme and ordered that all TSR-2s on the production line and even the jigs were to be destroyed. Three aircraft were sent to

Above *TSR-2 XR219 showing all its aerodynamic sleekness* (Ashley Annis).

Shoeburyness as gunnery targets and two others were reduced to some major parts for the RAF Museum and the Cranfield Institute.

The TSR-2's replacement, the F-111, was later cancelled by the same government for reasons of cost.

BOEING B-9

Type: *Light bomber;* **Crew:** *Four;* **Manufacturers:** *Boeing Airplane Co, Seattle, Washington* **(YIB-9A)** **Powerplant:** *Two Pratt & Whitney R-1860-11;* **Dimensions:** *Span, 76 ft 10 in (23.20 m); Length, 52 ft (15.85 m); Height, 12 ft (3.65 m);* **Weights:** *Empty, 8,941 lb (4,064 kg); Loaded, 14,320 lb (6,509 kg);* **Performance:** *Max speed, 186 mph (299.5 km/h); Ceiling, 20,750 ft (6,326 m);* **Armament:** *Two machine-guns 2,400 lb (1,090 kg) bomb load.*

Boeing Models 214 and 215, which became the US Army Y1B-9 and YB-9, were logical military developments of the all-metal Boeing Model 221 Monomail mail/cargo aircraft, which first flew in May 1930. Boeing embarked on the two B-9 projects as a private venture in anticipation of their producing the same performance advance in the area of heavy bombers as the Monomail had done in the commercial sector.

The Models 214 and 215 embodied the same structural and aerodynamic refinement as the Monomail. Despite having open cockpits and a 2,200 lb (10,000 kg) bomb load being carried externally, the B-9 raised the speed of bombers to a point 5 mph (8.05 km/h) above that of contemporary fighters. The Model 215 (YB-9), powered by 600 hp Pratt & Whitney Hornet engines, was completed first and made its

A Boeing Y1B-9A in flight accompanied by a P-26A (Boeing).

maiden flight on 13 April 1931. Designated XB-901 by the US Army, this experimental model flew for the first time on 29 April 1931. Two months later the XB-901 was delivered to Wright Field for a thorough evaluation and an average speed of 158 mph (252.8 km/h) was achieved during a long flight across the USA with only two refuelling stops.

Model 214 (Y1B-9), originally powered with 600 hp liquid-cooled Curtis Conqueror engines, was changed to Hornet powerplant following US Army tests. A service test order for five aircraft (Boeing Model 246) was placed in August 1931 under the designation of Y1B-9A, and the two prototypes were purchased simultaneously. Although not ordered in quantity, the B-9 proved a major advance in bomber design. It also greatly influenced the Model 247, the first airliner produced in quantity by Boeing.

BOEING B-17 FLYING FORTRESS

Type: *Medium bomber*; **Crew:** *Nine*; **Manufacturers:** *Boeing Aircraft Co, Seattle, Washington; Douglas Aircraft Co, Long Beach, California; Lockheed Vega Aircraft Corp, Burbank, California;* **Powerplant:** *Four Wright R-1820-97*; **Dimensions:** *Span, 103 ft 9 in (31.6 m); Length, 74 ft 4 in (22.7 m); Height, 19 ft 1 in (5.8 m);* **Weight:** *Empty, 36,130 lb (16,422 kg); Loaded, 55,000 lb (25,000 kg);* **Performance:** *Max speed, 287 mph (462 km/h) at 25,000 ft (7,622 m); Ceiling 35,600 ft (10,854 m);* **Armament:** *13 .5 calibre machine-guns. Maximum bomb load, 12,800 lb (5,800 kg).*

In August 1934 the Boeing Company was invited to participate in a US Army competition for a new multi-engine bomber. The aircraft had to be capable of carrying a bomb load of 2,000 lb (909 kg) for between 1,020-2,200 miles (1,642-3,542 km) at a speed of 200-250 mph (322-402 km/h). The US Army stipulated that a flying prototype had to be available for trials in August 1935.

The term multi-engine had generally been used to indicate two engines. Boeing were already working on a new concept for a four-engined bomber and the XB-15 was currently under development for an Army contract so after obtaining assurances that it could submit an aircraft with additional engines in the competition, design work and construction were rushed ahead on a four-engined aircraft.

While the role of later versions was to be offensive, the Model 299 was conceived for a purely defensive mission; the protection of the American coastline from foreign surface fleets. It was this designation, and not the later, formidable defensive machine-gun armament, which suggested the famous name Flying Fortress.

Unlike its predecessor, the B-9, the XB-15 carried all bombs internally and defensive armament was comprised of four streamlined machine-gun blisters on the sides, top and bottom of the fuselage and a nose gunner's station. The prototype was powered by four 750 hp Pratt & Whitney Hornet engines. Rushed to completion in only a year, the Model 299 was taken into the air for the first time on 28 July 1935 by Boeing test pilot, Leslie Tower.

The Model 299 was flown from Seattle to Wright Field at Dayton, Ohio, only a month after the roll out. Average speed for the 2,100 mile (3,381 km) flight was an unbelievable 233 mph (375 km/h). The competitive testing was almost completed when on 30 October 1939 the Model 299 crashed following take-off with the controls inadvertently locked. Leslie Tower and Major Ployer Hill (chief of Wright flight testing) were killed, but three other crew members in the rear fuselage escaped. Before the crash, the US Army had been considering an order for 65 bombers. This was now reduced to a service test order for 13 flight articles and a static test model under the designation YB-17 — changed to Y1B-17 shortly before the first was ready for test flying on 2 December 1936. The major change from the Model 299 was the substitution of Wright Cyclone engines of 1,000 take-off horsepower for the earlier Hornets.

Boeing B-17Gs of the 381st Bomb Group, 8th Air Force, Ridgewell, England, in formation (USAF).

The first Y1B-17s went into service during January-August 1937 with the 2nd Bombardment Group. Meanwhile, the US Army ordered the static test aircraft completed as a high-altitude bomber with turbo-supercharged engines. This was delivered as the Y1B-17A and resulted in a production order for 39 B-17Bs. These were delivered to the 2nd and 7th Bomb Groups during October 1939-March 1940.

The B-17C, which flew for the first time on 21 July 1940, was a more combat-worthy model following recommendations made by Britain and France as a result of their battle experiences. Limited vision cupolas on the side of the fuselage were replaced with streamlined Plexiglas coverings and a single .50 calibre machine-gun was installed in the under-gunner's position. Armour plate and self-sealing fuel tanks were incorporated as a result of bitter experience in the European war. In the spring of 1941, 20 aircraft of a 1939 contract for 38 B-17Cs were delivered to Great Britain

where the type was converted for service as the Fortress I.

These aircraft were intended as trainers pending deliveries of the B-17E and were not to be used operationally. However, the aircraft situation in Britain at this time was acute and in June 1941 five Fortress Is were delivered to No 90 Squadron at Polebrook for high-altitude bombing operations. Three aircraft from this unit took part in a daylight raid on Wilhelmshaven on 8 July, and a further 23 operations followed during the summer of 1941.

By September it was decided that the Fortress was unsuitable for further operations with Bomber Command. Although it was an extremely well-built aircraft, operational experience revealed that its defensive fire-power of five machine-guns, was totally inadequate for flights over heavily defended targets in Europe. The RAF operated the Fortress I at altitudes approaching 30,000 ft (9,144 m). In 51 sorties, 26 were flown with no bombs being dropped. Bomb aimers did not feel able to drop their bombs accurately (the then top secret Norden bomb sight had been deleted from all 20 models supplied to the RAF). As a result of the

Inset left B-17Gs of the 96th Bomb Group, 8th Air Force at Snetterton Heath, Norfolk, prepare to take off for a raid over Germany in 1944 (USAF).

Inset below B-17E Yankee pictured during the last years of America's peace in 1941 (USAF).

Background photograph B-17G 42-97246, one of 4,035 G models which were built. Unlike previous models, it carried a ball turret under the fuselage and a chin turret in the nose for added firepower (Boeing).

RAF experience, the 42 B-17Ds were built with self-sealing fuel tanks and minor refinements. The remaining B-17C models were modified to B-17D standard.

Results of the European combat experience were incorporated into the extensively improved B-17E which was ordered on 30 August 1940 and first flew on 5 September 1941. Power-operated gun turrets and a tail-gun position were installed and the .30 calibre guns were replaced with .50 calibre guns. The most distinctive recognition feature of the B-17E was its greatly enlarged tail surfaces which gave better control and stability for high-altitude bombing. About 100 B-17Es had been delivered to the US Army Air Corps by the time of the Japanese attack on Pearl Harbor on 7 December 1941. A handful of bomb groups fought the Japanese in the Philippines and Java and the survivors retreated to India. The B-17 continued to operate in the Pacific theatre until 1943.

Of 512 B-17Es built, 45 Fortress IIAs were delivered to the UK. Many gave sterling service to RAF Coastal Command where they helped close the mid-Atlantic 'gap'. The first B-17Es of the 97th Bomb Group landed in Britain in July 1942 and this unit flew the first American Fortress mission on 17 August.

Large-scale production really began with the B-17F, which could be distinguished outwardly from the B-17E by a moulded Plexiglas nose. Boeing built 2,300, and 600 and 500 each were delivered by Douglas and Lockheed-Vega respectively, in new factories built specially for the purpose.

At the start of 1943 the 8th Air Force in Britain had only four B-17F groups; approximately some 200 aircraft. On 27 January the 8th bombed Germany for the first time when B-17Fs of the 306th BG attacked Wilhelmshaven. During mid-July, hundreds of B-17Fs were used in a week of attacks beginning on 24 July which came to be known as 'Blitz Week'. Despite high losses the B-17s were despatched to Schweinfurt and Regensburg a month later, on 17 August. Sixty B-17s were

lost and many others written off in crashes in England; an unacceptable 19 per cent loss rate. On 6 September 45 B-17s failed to return from a raid on Stuttgart. The worst day, 'Black Thursday', occurred on 14 October, when another 60 B-17s were lost, again on a mission to Schweinfurt.

The final production version of the B-17 was the G, with an added two-gun power operated 'chin' turret under the nose for the defence against direct frontal attack. Boeing built 4,035 B-17Gs and Douglas and Lockheed built 2,395 and 2,250, respectively. At the peak of B-17 production in June 1944, the Boeing Seattle factory was rolling out 16 Fortresses every 24 hours.

The B-17G first began to equip bomb groups of the 8th Air Force in England in late 1943 while the 15th AF in Italy had to wait a little longer. The arrival of the P-51 Mustang enabled 1,000-plane raids deep into Germany. During March 1944 the first American raids on Berlin took place. By April 1944 the 8th could call upon almost 1,000 B-17Gs and the number was to double by August that year. By the time hostilities in Europe finished in May 1945,

almost 300,000 Fortress missions had taken place from Britain.

In post-war years, B-17s carrying droppable lifeboats were designated B-17H. A number were diverted to the US Navy as PB-1Ws for anti-submarine and weather reconnaissance flights and to the US Coast Guard as PB-1Gs. Wartime reconnaissance versions, originally known as F-9, were re-designated RB-17G.

After replacement as standard bombers, B-17s remained in service as trainers and VIP transports. Some were converted to radio-controlled targets and the last B-17 in US military service, a QB-17 drone, was destroyed in 1960, ironically, by a Boeing Bomarc missile. Following military service, some B-17s were used as 'borate bombers', extinguishing forest fires through the USA. Some of the survivors can be seen regularly on the air show circuit in America and around the world.

B-29 Censored of the 39th Bomb Group taxiing out at North Field, Guam. This Group flew its first mission to Maug, in the northern Marianas, early in April 1945 (USAF).

BOEING B-29 SUPERFORTRESS

Type: *Medium bomber;* **Crew:** *Ten;* **Manufacturers:** *Boeing Airplane Co, Seattle and Renton, Washington; Wichita, Kansas. Bell Aircraft Corp, Atlanta, Georgia. Glenn L Martin Co, Baltimore, Maryland;* **Powerplant:** *(B-29A) Four Wright R-335-23;* **Dimensions:** *Span, 14 ft 3 in (43.05 m); Length, 99 ft (30.2 m); Height, 29 ft 7 in (9.05 m);* **Weight:** *Empty, 74,500 lb (33,795 kg); Loaded, 135,000 lb (61,240 kg);* **Performance:** *Max speed, 357 mph (575 km/h) at 30,000 ft (9,144 m); Ceiling, 36,000 ft (10,973 m);* **Armament:** *20,000 lb (9,090 kg) bomb load.*

In 1938, initial studies were carried out by Boeing for an improved B-17 bomber with a pressurized cabin. There was then no 'official military requirement' for such a concept but Boeing continually updated the design until, in February 1940, an official requirement was issued to four companies for a high altitude bomber capable of carrying 2,000 lb (909 kg) of bombs a distance of 5,333 miles (8,587 km) with a speed of 400 mph (644 km/h). Although the Boeing Model 345 could only manage a projected speed of 382 mph, in every other respect it reigned

supreme and the XB-29 became the Superfortress.

From the start the Boeing pedigree was evident in the large, sleek bomber design which incorporated a high aspect wing, engine nacelles designed to minimize drag and a tricycle undercarriage fitted with dual wheels. The Wright R-3350 engines, with two superchargers, developing 2,200 horsepower at sea level, were the most powerful powerplants installed in an aircraft at that time. The fuselage was divided into three pressurized compartments, two of which were connected by a tunnel over the tandem bomb bays. The forward pressurized area contained the pilots, navigator, bombardier, flight engineer and radio operator, while the aft section housed three gunners and a radar operator. The tail gunner had his own separate pressurized compartment. The B-29 was far ahead of its contemporaries with ten-gun defensive armament in four remotely controlled power turrets and a single directly controlled tail turret.

Two prototypes were ordered on 24 August 1940 and designated XB-29 while a third was ordered in December that year along with a static test specimen. Construction of the prototype aircraft began in April 1941 at the Boeing Seattle plant. With American involvement in the war becoming almost a reality, the B-29 became the subject of an unprecedented large order for an as yet unproven design. A US Army test batch of 14 YB-29s was ordered, followed, in September 1941, by a production contract for 250 B-29s.

Following the Japanese attack on Pearl Harbor, American military strategists realized the importance of the long-range bomber to strike at targets in the Pacific and in January 1942 a contract for a further 250 B-29s was issued. The Boeing Wichita plant was later expanded and a new factory at Renton was given over entirely to B-29 production. Further production lines were started by Bell at Marietta, Georgia

B-29A-5-BN 42-93869, one of 1,119 B-29s built at the Boeing Renton plant (Boeing).

and by Martin at Omaha.

The first XB-29 was flown at Seattle by Edward Allen on 21 September 1942 and the second on 28 December 1942. There followed a spate of engine failures and fires and in February 1943 an engine fire caused the second XB-29 to crash, killing Allen, his crew and 19 civilian workers. Faults were rectified and the Sperry remotely-controlled gun turrets fitted to the second XB-29 were replaced by General Electric turrets in the third, which first flew in June 1943.

On 1 June 1943, the 58th Very Heavy Bombardment Wing was activated and the first seven YB-29s were delivered to this unit in July. By the end of 1943 it was decided that the B-29 would equip the newly formed 20th Bomber Command in India and China for raids on Japanese targets.

The first B-29 mission occurred on 5 June 1944 when their landing fields in China were used as staging posts to refuel and rearm for the strike on railway targets in Bangkok. Of the 98 B-29s which took off on the 2,000 mile (3,218 km) round trip. 14 aborted, and five crashed on landing. Only 18 bombs landed in the target area. Ten days later, 47 B-29s made a night attack on the Imperial Iron and Steel

Works at Yawata on the island of Kyushu. Seven B-29s were lost but, significantly, it was the first raid on the Japanese mainland. During the summer, five B-29 bases were constructed in the newly captured Marianas where it was decided to concentrate all the B-29s of the 20th Air Force. It was from here on 24 November 1944 that the first raid on Tokyo took place when Brigadier General O'Donnell's 73rd Wing bombed the Musashima aircraft factory.

Throughout late 1944 and early 1945, the B-29s carried out high level daylight raids on Japanese targets without success and at high cost. In March 1945, Major General Curtis E. LeMay decided that as the B-29s could not hit their targets accurately, they must area bomb using incendiaries to burn up large areas of Japanese towns and cities in an attempt to wreck the Japanese war effort. All Japan came to fear the dreaded 'Bni-Jus' (B-29s).

As enemy fighter opposition diminished, it was possible to improve the speed of the B-29 by deleting gun turrets and sighting blisters. These stripped versions were designated B-29B, B-29A having been assigned to Renton-built aircraft which featured a different type of centre wing construction. The new Superforts carried out low-level, individual

Left *Two famous Boeing aircraft; the B-17 and B-52, pictured at the 1986 RAF Mildenhall air fête.*

Right *Boeing Washington BI (ex-mothballed USAF B-29 44-61599) on arrival at RAF Marham in March 1950 where No 149 Squadron became the first RAF Squadron to be equipped with the type (Boeing).*

night bombing raids with fire bombs. On 9 March, 334 B-29s fire-bombed the capital. Almost 16 square miles of Tokyo was razed to the ground as gusting winds whipped up the flames and over 80,000 Japanese died. Fourteen B-29s were lost and 42 received varying degrees of flak damage. LeMay scheduled a further five fire bomb missions in ten days.

Throughout early 1945, B-29s based on Saipan, Tinian and Guam continued bombing Japanese targets. For attacks on oil refineries, B-29s of the 315th Bomb Wing based on Guam were stripped of all armament, except the tail turret, and AN/APQ-7 Eagle radar bomb sights were installed. The radar aerial was housed in a 14 ft (4.3 m) 'wing' under the fuselage. Another unit, the 313th carried out highly successful aerial mining of Japanese home waters and shipping lanes.

Despite the effective blockade and relentless bombing by an ever-increasing number of B-29s—by May 1945 LeMay had four wings and up to 500 Superfortresses under his command—Japan refused to surrender. Preparations began at Tinian for the possibility of B-29s delivering atomic bombs on Japanese cities. On 6 August Colonel Paul Tibbetts, CO of the 509th Composite Group, took off in

B-29 *Enola Gay* and, with six other B-29s, headed for Hiroshima. At 08:15 the 9,700 lb atomic bomb was released from a height of 31,600 ft (9,634 m). Tibbets pulled away sharply in a 155° turn to escape the glare and blast. The destruction was on an unprecedented scale (some 48,000 buildings were destroyed) and although 78,000 Japanese people died in the explosion, it was actually fewer than in the first great B-29 fire raid against Tokyo, when 80,000 died.

No official reaction was received from the Japanese government, so on 9 August B-29 *Bocks Car*, piloted by Major Sweeney, headed for Kokura. On board Sweeney carried *Fat Man*, a plutonium device and the only remaining atomic device then in existence. Patchy cloud saved Kokura and *Fat Man* was released over Nagasaki, the secondary target. An estimated 35,000 people died in the conflagration.

Japan surrendered five days later, on 14 August. Overhead a record 804 B-29 Superfortresses bombed targets in Japan. The official surrender ceremony took place aboard USS *Missouri* in Tokyo Bay on 2 September. By then the B-29s had substituted bombs for food supplies and clothing parcels as the majority of

these aircraft flew mercy missions to thousands of beleaguered Allied prisoners of war scattered throughout the crumbling Japanese empire.

Altogether, 3,970 B-29s had been built when production ceased in 1946: 2,766 by Boeing, 668 by Bell and 536 by Martin. The end of the war resulted in the cancellation of an additional 5,092 B-29s on order.

With the end of the Second World War, Britain's armed force suffered a serious decline in manpower and equipment. As a stopgap measure, 70 (later increased to 88) B-29s were ordered under the Marshall Aid programme. Deliveries were begun in March 1950, although these were ex-USAF B-29s and B-29As which had been mothballed since the end of the war. In July 1950, the modernized B-29s which had reached the UK were named Washington and No 149 Squadron at Marham became the first unit to equip with the type, some two years after the first Tu-4 (Soviet B-29 copy) squadron had become operational in Russia. By the end of 1954 the English Electric Canberra had begun to replace the Washington in RAF service

TB-29A-45-BN, which flew 105 missions over Korea, was ferried from China Lake USN Base, California, to Duxford in 1980 and re-painted in its original Korean War markings of 44-61748, 307th Bomb Group, FEAF.

and most were returned to the USA.

An entirely new career was opened for the B-29 with the advent of aerial refuelling as means of extending the range of bombers and fighters. Under the designation KB-29M, 72 B-28s were converted at Wichita to flying tankers with a single large fuel tank filling each bomb bay, a hose that could be unreeled and secured to the receiver airplane and transfer pumps. Seventy-four B-29s were modified to receive fuel by this method, with one bomb bay used for increased fuel capacity.

The B-50A *Lucky Lady II* made the first nonstop flight around the world in 1949 after being refuelled by six KB-29Ms at three points *en route*. 116 B-29s were modified at Renton as KB-29P 'flying-boom' tankers.

The last B-29s in squadron service were retired in September 1960.

BOEING B-47 STRATOJET

Type: *Strategic medium bomber;* **Crew:** *Three;* **Manufacturers:** *Boeing Airplane Co, Seattle, Washington and Wichita, Kansas; Douglas Aircraft Co, Tulsa; Lockheed Aircraft Corp, Marietta, Georgia;* **Powerplant:** *(B-47E) Six General Electric J-47;* **Dimensions:** *Span, 116 ft (35.3 m); Length, 109 ft 10 in (33.3 m); Height, 27 ft 11 in (8.26 m);* **Weight:** *Empty, 80,756 lb (36,707 kg); Loaded, 206,700 lb (93,954 kg);* **Performance:** *Max speed, 606 mph (975 km/h) at 16,300 ft (4,969 m); Ceiling, 40,500 ft (12,347 m);* **Armament:** *Two 20 mm M24A1 cannon, 20,000 lb (9,090 kg) bomb load.*

Boeing development of a jet bomber began in 1943 when the first preliminary requirement was issued by the US Army. In March 1944, Boeing submitted the Model 424. It had straight wings, a fuselage and tail which owed much to the B-29 and engines paired in nacelles. At the end of the war, German wartime research into jet aircraft design was studied by the Allies and the results influenced the final Boeing design. A 35° swept-back wing that permitted great speed increases was incorporated in the Model 448 of September 1945 which proposed housing four engines in the forward fuselage and two in the rear fuselage.

By the time the mock-up of the Boeing Model 450 was approved in April 1946, the B-47 had moved even further from the conventional configuration. The six engines were now concentrated in two dual and two single underwing pods. A tandem 'bicycle' landing gear was adopted and a retractable outrigger wheel was mounted in each inboard jet pod for lateral ground stability. Because of the location of the main wheels relative to the centre of gravity, the B-47 sat on the ground in take-off attitude and took and landed at the same angle without 'rotating' in the traditional manner of aircraft

46-065 was the first of the two Boeing XB-47 prototypes to fly, leaving Boeing Field, Seattle, for Moses Lake AFB on 17 December 1947 (Boeing).

Above *In 1953, two B-47Bs were converted for trials with the British developed probe and drogue refuelling system, the receiver aircraft being re-designated YB-47F (50-009) (Boeing).*

with conventional landing gear. In May, two prototype XB-47s were ordered, the first of which flew from Boeing Field, Seattle to nearby Moses Lake AFB on 17 December 1947.

Because of its high wing loading and the slow acceleration characteristics of the early turbojet engines, 18 JATO rocket units were built into the sides of the fuselage. On later models these units were carried on a jettisonable external rack as a weight-saving measure. The heavy weight of these units also resulted in faster landing speeds and a severe braking problem, which was solved by the deployment of a ribbon-type parachute from the tail just as the wheels touched the ground.

Wartime experience with stripped-down B-29s had revealed that bombers with near fighter aircraft speeds could only be successfully intercepted from the rear, so the sole defensive armament of the B-47 was in the shape of tail turret guns that could be aimed and fired either remotely from the cockpit or automatically by radar.

The second XB-47 flew in July 1948 with the more powerful General Electric J47 powerplant of 5,200 lb (2,363 kg) of thrust in place of the

Above *Boeing B-47 23363 in Strategic Air Command livery* (Boeing).

Left *Boeing B-47 Stratojet 91909 with JATO rocket launchers on the sides* (Boeing).

earlier J35s of only 3,750 lb (1,705 kg) of thrust. The first of 10 Wichita-built B-47As flew in June 1950. Major production began with the B-47B, which flew for the first time at Wichita on 26 April 1951, and this version differed from the B-47A in having underwing drop tanks and J47 engines of 5,800 lb (2,636 kg) of thrust.

The RB-47 reconnaissance bomber was built with eight cameras in a removable bomb bay package. The B-47B was also built in small quantities by Douglas and Lockheed. The B-47B entered service with Strategic Air Command in mid-1951 when the type began equipping the 306th (Medium) Bomb Wing.

The designation B-47C was assigned to an experimental four-jet model that was not completed. The two XB-47Ds were Bs converted to flying test beds for Curtiss Wright T49 turboprop engines, at the time the most powerful ever to fly. Largest production series was the B-47E, which flew for the first time on 30 January 1953. The RB-47E version, of which 255 were delivered to Strategic Air Command, was easily identified by its extended nose that contained photographic equipment.

The YDB-47E was a special conversion used to air launch the Bell GAM-63 'Rascal' missile, which was then guided to the target under radio control by an operator in the YDB-47E. QB-47Es were radio-controlled, pilotless drones used as aerial targets to test interceptor missiles against high performance aircraft.

The YB-47F and the single KB-47G were B-47Bs converted as a hose receiver to test the suitability of the hose-and-drogue refuelling method for bombers. The ERB-47H and RB-47H were built in small numbers and were the last of over 1,300 Wichita-built B-47s completed in October 1956. Fitted with pressurized capsules in the bomb bay, the ERB-47H had a five-man crew and the RB-47H had a six-man crew. The YB-47J was a test-bed for a new radar bombing-navigation system and the dual-purpose RB-47Ks were RB-47Es converted for weather-reconnaissance as well as photographic missions.

In 1957 the majority of B-47s in bomber configuration were modified, principally by strengthening the wings to allow them to use the revolutionary low-level 'lob-bombing' technique with the bomb being released during a zooming vertical climb and the aircraft disengaging by completing a fighter tactic, the Immelman turn. The increased manoeuvrability gave the B-47 a mission to match what pilots described as a 'six-engine fighter'.

Above *Boeing B-52G, one of 193 built at Wichita, Kansas (Boeing).*

Right *Boeing B-52D of the 96th Bomb Wing comes into land at RAF Marham during the USAF-RAF bombing competition on 23 September 1981.*

BOEING B-52 STRATOFORTRESS

Type: *Strategic heavy bomber;* **Crew:** *Six;* **Manufacturers:** *Boeing Airplane Co, Seattle, Washington and Wichita, Kansas (B-52G);* **Powerplant:** *Eight Pratt & Whitney J57-P-43W turbojets;* **Dimensions:** *Span, 185 ft (56.4 m); Length, 15 ft 7 in (48 m); Height, 40 ft 8 in (12.4 m);* **Weight:** *Loaded, 488,000 lb (221,500 kg);* **Performance:** *Max speed, 630 mph (1,014 km/h) approximately at 24,000 ft (7,315 m); Ceiling, 55,000 ft (16,765 m); Range, 8,500 miles (13,680 km).*

Designed as a nuclear bomber the B-52 saw service in South-East Asia from 1965-73 and is still in first-line service today as a missile platform with the ability to fly in the 'closed curtain' environment. The designation B-52 was originally assigned in 1946 to a straight-wing, long-range bomber to be powered by six turbo-prop engines. By October 1948, the design had undergone extensive revision, and at that time the USAF approved Boeing's request to develop an entirely new jet-propelled bomber under the same designation. The new B-52 was designed and built as Boeing Model 464.

38

In appearance, the new bomber was a direct development of the B-47. Eight Pratt & Whitney J57 turbojet engines were carried in four pods under the wings and the four-unit tandem landing gear could be turned to either side to allow the aircraft to crab into the wind on crosswind landings and still roll straight down the runway. Electrical needs on early B-52s were handled by turbine powerpacks driven by air bled from the second stage compressors of the jet engines. Fuel was carried in fuselage tanks above the bomb bay and in nylon bladder cells installed between the main wing spars and each pair of interconnecting ribs.

Two prototypes, the XB-52 and YB-52, were built. The YB-52 flew for the first time on 15 April 1952, and the first of three production B-52As flew on 5 August 1954. The B-52 and all the subsequent B-52s differed from the X and Y models in having a redesigned nose in which the pilots sat side-by-side in a cabin instead of in tandem under a plastic canopy as in the B-47s. The fuel capacity of the B-52A was increased by the use of 1,000 gallon drop tanks under each wing and provision was made for flying-boom aerial refuelling.

Fifty B-52Bs were built as dual-purpose aircraft. A photo-reconnaissance or electronic countermeasures capsule, complete with operating personnel, could be installed in the bomb bay for specialized missions. When fitted with the capsule the aircraft was designated RB-52B. In 1955 it began to replace the B-36 as Strategic Air Command's primary heavy bomber. The B-52B entered service with Strategic Air Command on 29 June 1955, with the 93rd Heavy Bombardment Wing at Castle AFB, California.

On 9 March 1956, the first of 35 B-52Cs made its maiden flight. It, too, was a dual-purpose design, but was built to higher load factors and had a gross weight of 450,000 lb (204,545 kg). Fuel capacity was increased by the use of 3,000 gallon drop tanks. Deliveries to SAC began in June 1956 and during that month the first of 69 Wichita-built B-52Ds

Background photograph *Boeing B-52C, of which 35 were built, with 3,000 gallon drop tanks* (Boeing).

Inset right *Close-up of a 96th Bomb Wing B-52D tail gun installation at RAF Marham during the bombing competition on 23 September 1981.*

made their maiden flight. The longer-range
B-52D, which entered service with SAC in
December 1956, was used only as a bomber.
The first of 101 B-52Ds produced at Seattle
flew for the first time on 28 September 1956.
The B-52D was subsequently modified to carry
a maximum of 108 conventional bombs,
B-52D production was followed by 42 Seattle-
built B-52Es and with a further 58 being produced at Wichita. The B-52E, which entered
service with SAC in July 1957, introduced improvements in bombing, navigation and elec-
tronics systems.

Deliveries of the B-52F began in June 1958,
and in total 99 B-52Fs were produced at Seattle
and Wichita. The B-52F was fitted with
engine-driven alternators instead of pneumatic
powerpacks. Seattle production ended after 44
B-52Fs had been produced but the Wichita
plant went on to produce 193 B-52Gs and 102
B-52Hs. The final B-52H was received by SAC
in 1962. Outwardly, the 'G' and 'H' differ from
previous models in having a shortened vertical
tail. Internally, wing fuel bladders were replaced
by integral tanks. Two supersonic AGM-28
'Hound Dog' missiles can be carried. The
B-52H is fitted with TF-33 turbofan engines
for improved unrefuelled range and a General
Electric Vulcan 20 mm cannon in the radar-
directed tail turret.

The B-52G and B-52H are also equipped to
carry 20 AGM-69 supersonic Boeing short-
range attack missiles (SRAMs) (eight SRAMs
and four gravity bombs in the internal
weapons bay and 12 SRAMs externally under
the wings). In 1992, the B-1B will take over the
role of stand-off cruise missile launchers from
the B-52H, which in turn will replace the
B-52G in the bomber/minelayer role.

In all, some 744 B-52s have been built, including 467 at Wichita.

Above left *Boeing YB-52, one of two prototypes, which
flew on 15 April 1952 (Boeing).*

Left *Boeing B-52B, of which 50 were built as dual-purpose
aircraft for bombing or photo-reconnaissance/ECM missions
(Boeing).*

CONSOLIDATED B-24 LIBERATOR

Type: *Medium bomber;* **Crew:** *8-10;* **Manufac-
turers:** *Consolidated (later Consolidated-Vultee) Aircraft
Corporation, San Diego, California (B-24A-
D,F,J,L,M,P) and Fort Worth (B24D-E,H,J). Douglas
Aircraft Co, Tulsa, Oklahoma (B-24D-E,H,J). Ford
Motor Co, Willow Run, Michigan (B-24E,H-J,K,L-
N,Q). North American Aviation Inc, Dallas, Texas
(B-24G/J);* **Powerplant:** *(B-24H/J) Four Pratt &
Whitney R-1830-65 Twin-Wasps;* **Dimensions:** *Span,
110 ft (33.5 m); Length, 67 ft 2 in (20.47 m); Height,
18 ft (5.49 m);* **Weight:** *Empty, 37,000 lb (16,783 kg);
Loaded, 65,000 lb (29,484 kg);* **Performance:** *Max
speed, 290 mph (467 km/h) at 25,000 ft (7,621 m); Ceil-
ing, 28,000 ft (8,534 m); Range, 2,100 miles (3,381 km);*
Armament: *Ten .5 in machine-guns, 8,000 lb
(4,000 kg) bomb load.*

Although the Liberator enjoyed only a short
operational career, it was much more versatile
than its more famous rival, the B-17 Flying
Fortress, and it made a vital contribution towards winning the war in the Pacific. No other
American aircraft was built in greater numbers
or saw such widespread service. As well as form-
ing a unique and powerful arm of the US 8th
Air Force in Europe, in August 1943 Liberators
flying at low level attacked the Ploesti oilfields in
Romania, while in the Far East B-24s hauled
supplies across the 'Hump' from India into
China, re-supplying B-24 squadrons before
they could bomb enemy targets. In the Pacific
the US Navy and the US Air Forces put the B
-24 to excellent use and it proved the scourge
of Japanese shipping and land targets.

Early in 1939, the US Army Air Corps drew
up a requirement for a heavy bomber of in-
finitely better performance than the B-17, then
in production. They were looking for a bomber
with a greatly improved range, some 3,000
miles (4,831 km) with a top speed in excess of
300 mph (483 km/h) and a ceiling of 35,000 ft
(10,670 m). The Consolidated Corporation of
San Diego, California, had already completed
a series of design studies into such a bomber,
where the chief architect was Isaac Machlin

Laddon, who was responsible for the Catalina flying-boat. Consolidated had a reputation for building flying-boats and it earned the Liberator the nickname, 'banana boat' (mainly from B~17 crews).

In May 1938, the French Government had issued a specification to Consolidated for a heavy bomber. The company's early study designated LB~30, was a landplane version of their Model 29 flying-boat (PB2~Y), but interest shown by the Army Air Corps prompted a further design study designated XB~24, which incorporated David R. Davis's high-aspect-ratio wing and the twin-finned empennage used on the Model 31 flying-boat (P4Y~1).

By 20 January 1939, preliminary specifications of the Model 32 were ready, but Consolidated had to carry out almost 30 changes before the Air Corps would issue a contract for the XB~24 prototype, on 30 March 1939.

Consolidated B-24D Liberators. The nearest aircraft is 41-23852 (USAF).

Among the more unusual features was a tricycle undercarriage and the main gears had to be long to exceed the tall bomb bays and were retracted outwards by electric motors. Roller-shutter doors were fitted to protect the 8,000 lb (4,000 kg) bomb load which was stowed vertically in the two halves of the bomb bay. The XB~24 had hand-held .30 in Browning machine-guns in the nose, waist, dorsal and ventral positions and in the tail.

In September 1939, France followed up its tentative order with a production contract for 139 aircraft under the original LB~30 designation. On 26 October, the Davis wing was married to the fuselage for the first time and on 29 December the XB~24 made its maiden flight. William A. Wheatley was at the controls as it took off from Lindbergh Field next to the Consolidated plant in San Diego. (On 2 June 1941 Wheatley was killed during the final acceptance flight of the Liberator Mk II for the RAF.)

In 1940, a contract was placed for seven

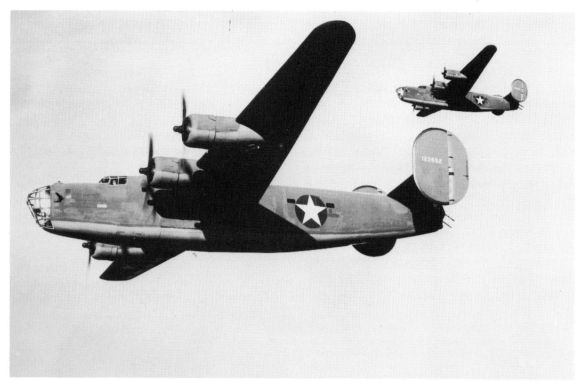

Consolidated B-24J Liberators of the 409th Bomb Squadron, 93rd Bomb Group, 2nd Air Division, 8th Air Force encountering flak en route to Augsburg, 1 March 1945 (USAF).

YB-24s for Service trials in the autumn. These aircraft were similar to the XB-24, but the gross weight had been increased by 5,400 lb (2,454 kg) to 46,400 lb (21,090 kg), the wing leading edge slots deleted and de-icing boots fitted to the wings and tail. Later that year, a further order was placed for 36 of the initial B-24 production version. However, only nine aircraft were completed to B-24A standard, which now weighed 53,600 lb (24,363 kg) and had .5 in machine-guns in the tail in place of the .30 in guns of previous models.

Six YB-24s and 20 B-24As were diverted to the RAF and after the fall of France in June 1940, Britain took over the French contract for 139 LB-30s. As a result of experience gained in Europe in other combat types, the XB-24 was fitted with self-sealing fuel tanks and armour plate.

Meanwhile, in 1941, Consolidated developed the RB-24B, fitted with turbo-supercharged Pratt & Whitney R-183-41 engines replacing the mechanically supercharged 33s. The substitution was marked with the relocation of the oil coolers on each side of the radial engines instead of underneath, and this produced the characteristic elliptical cowling seen on all subsequent models. The aircraft underwent further cosmetic changes with the installation of a Martin dorsal turret and a Consolidated-built tail turret. A further nine of the 1940 consignment of 36 were completed in 1941 as B-24Cs.

On 17 January 1941, the first Liberator for the RAF made its maiden flight and the first production models began flying the Atlantic in March that year. Six were diverted for service as transports on the embryonic Trans-Atlantic Return Ferry Service route between Montreal, Newfoundland and Prestwick. At first they were flown by BOAC crews and, later, by RAF Ferry Command pilots. These unarmed transport Liberators were designated LB-30A, which was the equivalent to the Liberator I, and later examples, LB-30B, equivalent to the Liberator II. In August 1941, deliveries to the RAF of the 139 aircraft on the original French contract began and by December that year 65 had been delivered to Britain. In September 1941 Liberator Is entered service with Coastal Command of the RAF and in June 1942 the Liberator entered RAF service in the bomber role.

The first significant version to see service with the USAAF was the B-24D. It was basically similar to the B-24C but had uprated engines and the gross weight now stood at 56,000 lb (25,000 kg). Contracts awarded in 1940 and subsequent orders brought the number of B-24Ds built by 1941 to 2,738, of which 2,425 were constructed by Consolidated-Vultee at San Diego. In RAF service the B-24D became the Liberator III and was

supplied under direct British contracts. The Liberator IIIA and subsequent versions were supplied under Lend-Lease and handed over to the RAF by the USAAF. A later series used in RAF service, B-24D, was designated the Liberator Mark V, equipped with additional fuel tanks in wing bays and centimetric Air to Surface Vessel (ASV) radar, either in a retractable radome in the ventral position aft of the bomb bays or in the chin. B-24Ds had already been supplied to the RCAF in September 1943 and 12 others went to the Royal Australian Air Force in 1944. The RCAF Liberators were similar to the RAF Mark III, but the RAF version usually had the Consolidated tail turret replaced by a Boulton Paul one with four .303 in machine guns.

PB4Y-1 Navy versions of the B-24D began reaching operational units late in 1942 and one claimed the first success against a U-boat on 5 November that year. In August 1943 the USAAF transferred all its B-24-equipped, anti-submarine squadrons to the US Navy. Anti-Submarine Command was disbanded and all

B-24H 42-95378 of the 726th Bomb Squadron, 451st Bomb Group, 15th Air Force, Italy (USAF).

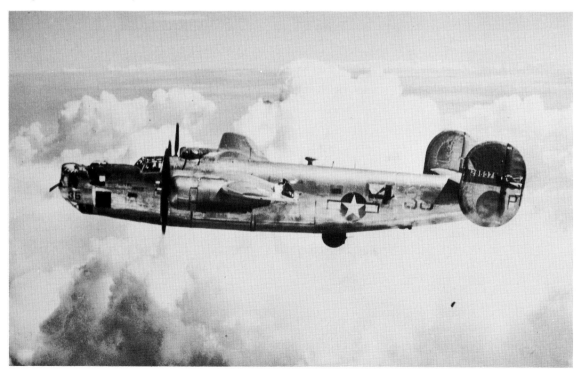

B-2D Liberators of the 93rd Bomb Group over England in 1943. The nearest aircraft is Joisey Bounce *a veteran of the Ploesti oil strike on 1 August 1943 (USAF).*

ASV-equipped B-24Ds were handed over to the US Navy as PB4Y-1s in exchange for an equal number of unmodified B-24s already in production for the Navy. Ultimately, the US Navy was to receive a total of 977 PB4Y-1s. Outwardly, they differed little from the USAAF model, although some, equivalent to the B-24J, were fitted with Erco bow turrets.

During 1942, a second Liberator production line was opened at Fort Worth, Texas where Convair turned out 303 B-24Ds. A third production line was started at Tulsa, where the Douglas Company produced ten B-24Ds before changing production to B-24Es. The B-24E was similar to the B-24D but had different propellers. At the end of 1942 a fourth B-24 production line was opened, by the Ford Motor Company at Willow Run. The first B-24 rolled out of its doors was a Consolidated model re-assembled at Willow Run from the sub-assemblies of two aircraft shipped from San Diego.

Early in 1943, the fifth and final major Liberator plant was operated by North American at Dallas, Texas. Its first 430 B-24s were designated 'G', the first 25 being very similar to the B-24D. The remainder introduced a nose turret containing two .50 in machine-guns built by Emerson and Consolidated after experience of head-on attacks made on the glass-nosed B-24Ds in Europe. The B-24G served only with the 15th Air Force in Italy. Variants similar to the 'G' were built by Consolidated at Fort Worth and by Douglas and Ford as the B-24H. Convair built 738 with Consolidated nose turrets while Douglas built 582 using Emerson turrets. Ford built 1,780 B-24Hs which were fitted with nose turrets similar to the Consolidated model and a further 1,587 B-24Js which were similar in appearance to the

B-24H but had a Motor Products nose turret and later autopilot and bomb sight. Altogether, 6,678 B-24Js were built by all five Liberator plants, the greatest number of all Liberator variants.

In November 1943, deliveries of the B Mark VI and GR Mark VI Liberators to the RAF were begun. These versions were Convair built B-24H and 'J' models with American turrets except for the tail turret which was by Boulton Paul. The GR Mark VI anti-submarine aircraft later incorporated a radome containing centimetric radar in place of the ball turret. By the end of the war over 1,800 Mark VIs and VIIIs had been used by the RAF, RCAF and RAAF.

In the Middle East the Mark VI was used mainly against enemy shipping in the Mediterranean. Beginning in late 1944, 36 Mark VIIIs were delivered to the RAF in that theatre, each equipped with centimetric radar designed for Pathfinder (PFF) operations against ground targets. In the Far East the Mark VI was the principal bomber used in the final Burma campaign ending with the capture of Rangoon. Towards the end of 1944, 6,000 B-24s were on operational strength with the USAAF, equipping some 45 groups worldwide.

The last combat models of note were the B-24L and the B-24M. The B-24L differed from previous models primarily in the installation of a Convair-designed tail station which incorporated two hand-held .50 in machineguns. Consolidated built 417 B-24Ls at San Diego, while Ford turned out 1,250 at Willow Run. These two factories were the only plants to build the B-24M, of which 916 were manufactured by Convair and 1,677 by Ford.

By the end of the Second World War almost 2,500 of one type or another had been delivered to the RAF and Commonwealth Air Forces, of which 1,694 were supplied by Consolidated alone. More B-24s (18,188) were built than any other American aircraft of the period.

B-24s of the 458th Bomb Group, 2nd Air Division, 8th Air Force en route to their target over the Norfolk countryside in 1944 (USAF).

CONVAIR B-36

Type: *Heavy strategic bomber;* **Crew:** *15 including four reliefs;* **Manufacturers:** *Consolidated Vultee Aircraft Corporation, Fort Worth, Texas;* **Powerplant:** *(B-36J) Six Pratt & Whitney R-4360-53 pusher propeller engines and four General Electric J47-GE-19 turbojets;* **Dimensions:** *Span, 230 ft (70.1 m); Length, 162 ft 1 in (49.4 m); Height, 46 ft 8 in (14.3 m);* **Weight:** *Empty, 171,035 lb (77,743 kg); Loaded, 410,000 lb (186,36 kg);* **Performance:** *Max speed, 411 mph (661 km/h) at 36,400 ft (11,097 m); Ceiling, 39,900 ft (12,164 m); Range, 6,800 miles (10,950 km);* **Armament:** *Load of 72,000 lb (32,727 kg).*

For ten years, 1948-58, the Convair B-36 lived up to its unofficial name, 'Peacemaker', bridging the gap between the Boeing B-29 and the Boeing B-52 in service with Strategic Air Command as a truly intercontinental bomber. Although the B-36 never 'fired a shot in anger' it was instrumental in maintaining the peace during the Cold War of the early 1950s.

The Consolidated Aircraft Corporation began planning a very long-range bomber in 1940. Development began in the spring of 1941 when America considered the strong possibility of a bomber which could strike at European targets then under German domination. A specification issued in April 1941 called for an aircraft capable of carrying a 10,000 lb (4,545 kg) bomb load for 10,000 miles (16,103 km) and an operational ceiling of 35,000 ft (10,670 m). The sheer size of the aircraft would require a 5,000 ft (1,524 m) runway; almost an impossible task at the time.

The proposed Consolidated Model 37 was built around a six-engine pusher-type design and it was selected from among four designs submitted on 6 October 1941. On 15 November 1941 a contract was awarded for two prototypes. From the drawing board stage it was obvious that the new bomber would be bigger

Convair XB-36 42-13570 prototype which flew for the first time on 8 August 1946. This aircraft almost came to grief on its 16th test flight on 25 March 1947 when the right main gear retraction cylinder burst. Test pilots Erickson and Green landed the XB-36 safely after the crew had bailed out and fuel had been used (General Dynamics).

than anything hitherto designed. The sheer enormity of the project almost caused its downfall. In order to reach the original range specification the Model 37 would have to carry 21,116 gallons of fuel in the wings. Magnesium, plastics and new metals were employed to save weight. The Model 37 had an enormous wing span of 230 ft (70.1 m) and a fuselage length of 162 ft (49.3 m); far bigger than the B-52 which succeeded it.

In 1942, the B-36 project was transferred from Convair's San Diego Division to its Fort Worth plant, shortly after this mile-long bomber factory was erected and began producing B-24 Liberators. B-36 development was slow because of the demands made on the Convair Fort Worth plant for the B-24 Liberator but the project was revived in 1943 when plans were advanced for the bombing of the Japanese mainland from American bases. On 23 July 1943 a contract for 100 aircraft was placed.

RB-36F 49-2707 was involved in the Convair Tom-Tom project whereby two F-84 parasite fighters were connected to the mother ship through a direct wingtip to wingtip hook-up. The project was not a success and was terminated late in 1953. (General Dynamics).

The XB-36 was finally rolled out on 8 September 1945 and the prototype was first flown on 8 August 1946. Six R-4360-53 pusher-type piston engines drove 19 ft (5.79 m) diameter reversible-pitch propellers, which acted as a braking force during landing. These three-bladed, hollow-steel propellers had a built-in thermal de-icing system for all-weather operations. Leading edges of the B-36's wing and tail were double skinned to permit the flow of heated air for anti-icing. Heated air also defrosted the pilot's and bombardier's enclosures and their several sighting blisters.

The central portion of the 230 ft (70 m) wing was 7 ft 6 in (2.3 m) thick — high enough to

Bombers ancient and modern

Above *A Tu-20 Bear is closely shadowed by an F-4 Phantom of the US Navy (US Navy).*

Below *Avro Lancaster of the Battle of Britain Flight takes off from Mildenhall during the annual air fête. May 1985.*

Left *Avro Lancaster* City of Lincoln *in formation with Supermarine Spitfire IX on 30 August 1981.*

Below *TSR-2 XR222, the fourth prototype, as pictured at Cranfield in September 1977 (Harry Holmes).*

Above B-17Gs of the 91st Bomb Group, 8th Air Force during a daylight raid from Bassingbourn, England (USAF).

Right Unique formation of two F-111s and B-17 Sally B over Thorpe Abbotts, wartime home of the 100th Bomb Group, in October 1986.

Above *The North American B-25A Mitchell, which introduced self-sealing tanks and armour plate (USAF).*

Left *The last Avro Vulcan in flying condition being put through its paces on the airshow circuit in 1986.*

Below *Boeing B-52H of the 319th Bomb Wing at RAF Marham during the 'Giant Strike' bombing competition on 16 June 1981.*

Above B-17G Texas Raiders *of the Confederate Air Force during a pre-show warm up flight in October 1986.*

Right *F-111F of the 48th Tactical Fighter Wing coming in to land at its home base of RAF Lakenheath in October 1986.*

Below *Canberra B 2 WH725 with yellow and black Suez stripes on display at the Imperial War Museum at Duxford in 1984.*

Left *Early B-24D Liberators on a training flight in the USA (USAF).*

Right *Soviet Tu-16 Badger photographed from a US Navy interceptor (US Navy).*

Above *Victor K Mk 2 of No 57 Squadron pictured taking off from RAF Marham on 23 September 1981. 57 Squadron disbanded on 30 June 1986.*

Right *Hawker Hind which was brought overland to the UK from Afghanistan and restored by the Shuttleworth Trust to flying condition. Previously in Afghan markings, it is now painted in the colours of No 15 Squadron.*

Above *Junkers Ju 87 Stuka on display outside the RAF Museum.*

Below *Rockwell B-1B: one of the hundred supplied to the USAF between 1985 and 1988.*

permit installation of a catwalk so that crew members could climb into the wing for access to the engine nacelles in flight. Crews consisted of 16 men, including five relief members. To travel back and forth between the pressurized forward and aft compartments crewmen used a wheeled trolly on rails running through an 85 ft (25.9 m) pressurized tunnel.

The first production model was flown on 28 August 1947 and that month the first of some 22 unarmed B-36As were delivered to SAC. On 8 July 1948, the first of 73 B-36Bs made its first flight. This model differed from the B-36A in having six remotely controlled and retractable turrets containing two 20 mm cannon each and a further two 20 mm guns in fixed turrets in the nose and tail. It also had 3,500 hp engines in place of the 3,000 hp powerplants.

Early in 1949, the B-36 was the subject of a bitter inter-service argument between the US Navy and the USAF which resulted in a special Congressional Investigation into the combat effectiveness of the B-36. The aircraft was vindicated and the Admirals routed. The B-36D became 'six turning, four burning', with the introduction of four General Electric J-47-19 turbojets in two pods under the wings, and flew for the first time on 26 March 1949. Previously-built models were retrofitted with jetpods, snap-action bomb bay doors and various other improvements.

On 18 December 1949, the RB-36D variant of the B-36D flew for the first time. Externally, it closely resembled the B-36, but internally it carried a crew of 22 and 14 cameras were mounted in the forward bomb bay, including one with a 42 in focal length lens. The RB-36D entered service with SAC on 3 June 1950. Convair-Fort Worth modified a number of RB-36 reconnaissance bombers into carriers for RF-84 reconnaissance fighters, providing the USAF with the capability for long-range high-speed reconnaissance. The 'parasite' RF-84 swept-wing jet could be released and retrieved by the 'mother' RB-36 while in flight. This version was known as the GRB-36.

As part of a research and development pro-gramme on atomic-powered aircraft, a B-36 was modified to carry an operating atomic reactor in flight. Designated NB-36H, this aircraft conducted significant tests in shielding personnel and the effects of radiation on equipment.

The B-36F, which had 3,800 hp piston engines, flew for the first time on 18 November 1950. This was followed by the B-36H which introduced various refinements, including a two-station flight engineers' panel. The B-36H flew for the first time on 5 April 1952. Altogether, 81 Hs and 73 RB-36Hs were built. The B-36J had additional fuel tanks in the wings and a maximum gross weight of over 400,000 lbs. The first of 33 B-36Js flew for the first time on 3 September 1953.

Altogether, some 385 examples were built for SAC. The last B-36 was delivered to the USAF on 4 August 1954. The last B-36 was retired from the USAF on 12 February 1959, the day Strategic Bomber Command became an all-jet bomber force.

CONVAIR B-58 HUSTLER

Type: *Supersonic medium bomber;* **Crew:** *Three;* **Manufacturers:** *Convair Division of General Motors, Fort Worth, Texas;* **Powerplant:** *Four 15,600 lb (7,090 kg) (with afterburner) General Electric J79-GE-3B turbojets;* **Dimensions:** *Span, 56 ft 10 in (17.1 m); Length, 96 ft 9 in (29.54 m); Height, 31 ft 5 in (9.6 m);* **Weight:** *Loaded, 160,000 lb+ (72,727 kg);* **Performance:** *Max speed, 1,385 mph (2,230 km/h) at 40,000 ft (12,195 m); Service ceiling, 60,000 ft (18,292 m);* **Armament:** *One General Electric T-171E3 Vulvan 20 mm cannon with a radar-aimed tail mounting. Four wing-mounted pylons for a variety of weapons and a mission pod under aircraft centreline to carry nuclear or conventional bomb loads and fuel.*

Original Convair design studies for a manned supersonic bomber began in 1949. In January 1951, the company submitted a proposed design (Convair Model 4) to the USAF, and in 1952 orders were received for 30 test aircraft. The first of these was completed at Fort Worth on 31 August 1956, and 10 were later converted to B-58As, with another eight modified to dual control TB-58A trainers. The first of two XB-58s flew for the first time on 11 November 1956, with four General Electric J79-GE-1 turbojets. Each aircraft from the twelfth B-58 on was re-engined with the J79-GE-5A.

The Hustler's heat resistant skin and conical cambered delta wing was constructed of fibreglass, aluminium and stainless steel honeycomb sandwiched between two layers of metal. Miniaturization was employed where practical and many automatic systems made the task of operation and monitoring easier for the crew. The B-58 was the first aircraft to be built around a weapons system concept from the outset.

A feature of the B-58 was its droppable centreline pod which carried a portion of the aircraft's fuel supply and its nuclear payload. By March 1962 four pylons for underwing

weapons were fitted. From late 1963 a number of Hustlers were equipped with a BLU-2B dual pod (which was flown for the first time on 12 May 1960) containing a BA53-Y1 nuclear warhead and 4,000 gallons (18,184 litres) of fuel in the lower compartment. Optionally, the lower compartment could carry a photo-reconnaissance capability.

The Hustler went supersonic for the first time on 30 December 1956. On 5 June 1957 the first demonstration of a B-58 dropping its disposable pod, carried at Mach .91 cruising and released on a Mach 2 dash over the target at 55,000 ft (16,764 m), took place. On 29 June the B-58 made its first Mach 2 flight and on 18 September the bomber demonstrated low-level capabilities in a flight from Fort Worth, Texas to California, flying at almost 700 mph (1,127 km/h) at a maximum altitude of 500 ft (152 m) above the ground.

On 1 December 1959 the USAF took delivery of its first production model B-58A at Carswell AFB. On 15 March 1960 Strategic Air Command officially designated the 43rd Bomb Wing at Carswell as the first unit to

Convair B-58A Hustler 59-2456 in flight, showing its conventional underwing stores and fuel and weapons pod (Convair).

operate the B-58A. Later, on 23 March, a USAF crew completed the longest B-58 mission thus far, approximately 11,000 miles (17,713 km) at 620 mph (998 km/h) in 18 hours 10 minutes non-stop, with two air-to-air refuellings. In August the 43rd Bomb Wing's Hustlers became operational, and that same month SAC accepted its first TB-58 trainer. The only other unit in which the B-58 served was the 305th Bomb Wing, which began equipping in 1961.

Early accidents (nine of the first 30 aircraft crashed) and the introduction of the intercontinental ballistic missile (ICBM) into SAC (beginning in September 1960) were responsible for the B-58's short service life. Only 116 B-58s (including eight TB-58A trainers) were built, the last being delivered on 26 October 1962.

On 16 January 1970 the last Hustlers were retired from Strategic Air Command. Nevertheless, the B-58A was the first supersonic bomber to enter production for the USAF and the aircraft went on to set no less than 19 speed and altitude records.

DASSAULT-BREGUET MIRAGE IVA

Type: *Strategic bomber*; **Crew:** *Two*; **Manufacturers:** *Avions Marcel Dassault/Breguet Aviation*; **Powerplant:** *Two SNECMA Atar 9K turbojets*; **Dimensions:** *Span, 38 ft 10½ in (11.85 m); Length, 77 ft 1 in (23.5 m); Height, 17 ft 8½ in (5.4 m);* **Weight:** *Empty, 31,967 lb (14,500 kg); Loaded, 73,800 lb (33,475 kg);* **Performance:** *Max speed, 1,454 mph (2,340 km/h) at 40,000 ft (13,125 m), Ceiling, 65,620 ft (20,000 m);* **Armament:** *None. Provision for one Kiloton bomb or 16,000 lb (7,257 kg).*

In 1954 a decision was taken to provide France with its own nuclear strike deterrent force. At first the Vautour was considered, but Dassault started work on a bomber version of a 1956 company design for a twin-engined night fighter. In 1957 the design was dramatically modified so that two Pratt & Whitney J57B

Dassault-Breguet Mirage IVA supersonic nuclear bomber. (Dassault).

turbojets could be fitted to carry the new bomber to the easternmost borders of the Soviet Union.

Finally, two SNECMA Atar 9K turbojets were fitted and the design was scaled down with in-flight refuelling being selected as a means of completing the nuclear mission. With a range of barely 2,000 miles (3,220 km) the Mirage IVA relied heavily on extensive in-flight refuelling, sometimes using the 'buddy' technique whereby one Mirage IV would carry the bombload while the other refuelled it in flight. Fourteen KC-135FS stratotankers were delivered to France with the flying boom modified to trail a probe/drogue matched to the Mirage IVA.

The Mirage IV-001 flew for the first time on 17 June 1959 and was followed by the first production IVA, which made its maiden flight on 7 December 1963. Deliveries of some 62 Mirage IVs to the Armée de l'Air, Commandement des Forces Aèriennes Stratégic took place during 1964-March 1968. The type equips three Escadres which in turn are split into small groups dispersed over large areas. Quick action alert from unpaved strips can and has been undertaken using rocket assisted take-off.

In 1986-87 conversion of 18 Mirage IVA bombers to IVP standard with advanced avionics and modification to carry the ASMP nuclear missile took place. About 43 Mirage IVs are still in service and these will continue in the strike/reconnaissance role until 1996.

DE HAVILLAND DH 9A

Type: *Day bomber;* **Crew:** *Two;* **Manufacturers:** *Aircraft Manufacturing Co, Hendon; Westland Aircraft Ltd, Yeovil; F.W. Berwick & Co, London; Vulcan Motor & Engineering Co, Southport; Mann Egerton & Co, Norwich; Whitehead Aircraft Co, Richmond; Dayton-Wright Airplane Co, Dayton, Ohio: Engineering Division of the US Army Air Service, Ohio;* **Powerplant:** *Variously, one Rolls-Royce Eagle VIII, Liberty 12, Napier Lion or Napier Lion II;* **Dimensions:** *Span, 46 ft (14 m); Length, 30 ft (9.1 m); Height, 10 ft 9 in (3.3 m);* **Weight:** *Empty, 2,695 lb (1,225 kg); Loaded, 4,645 lb (2,111 kg);* **Performance:** *Max speed 114 mph (183.5 km/h) at 10,000 ft (3,048 m); Ceiling, 16,500 ft (5,030 m).*

The DH 9A, known familiarly as the 'Nineack', evolved from the disappointing DH 9 and was subsequently manufactured in quantity by

Above *De Havilland DH 9As of No 39 Squadron rehearsing for the Hendon Air Display, June 1926* (Hawker Siddeley).
Left *De Havilland DH 9As in the Middle East in 1919-20* (Norfolk & Suffolk Aviation Museum).

the Westland Aircraft Works in Yeovil. The 'Nine-ack' was originally designed as a replacement for the DH 9 with the Independent Force, RAF, and first entered service with No 110 Squadron in June 1918.

Almost 900 had been built by the end of the First World War and a further 300 were delivered to the RAF before production ceased in 1927. The DH 9A remained in service with the RAF until 1931. Throughout the 1920s the DH 9A, together with the Bristol Fighter, formed the backbone of the RAF in Iraq and India. From 21 June 1921, DH 9As of Nos 30 and 47 Squadrons were operated on the Cairo-Baghdad mail flight. In Iraq and northern India the tropicalized 'Nine-ack' became a general purpose aircraft fitted with an extra radiator and an overload fuel tank. In addition, 'Nine-acks' often carried spare wheels and goatskins filled with water during long policing actions far from base.

DE HAVILLAND MOSQUITO

Type: *Medium bomber;* **Crew:** *Two;* **Manufacturers:** *de Havilland Aircraft Co Ltd, Hatfield, Herts. Sub-Contracted by Airspeed, Percival Aircraft and Standard Motors, Canley;* **(IV) Powerplant:** *Two Rolls-Royce Merlin XXI;* **Dimensions:** *Span, 54 ft 2 in (16.5 m); Length, 40 ft 9½ in (12.5 m); Height, 15 ft 3½ in (4.66 m);* **Weight:** *Empty, 14,100 lb (6,409 kg); Loaded, 20,870 lb (9,486 kg);* **Performance:** *Max speed, 380 mph (612 km/h) at 17,000 ft (5,183 m); Ceiling, 28,800 ft (8,780 m);* **Armament:** *2,000 lb (9,090 kg) bomb load.*

It has been said that the bomber will always get through. The de Havilland Mosquito bomber is unique among Second World War aircraft in that it could and did, without the need for escort fighters which finally had to be used to protect the four-engined bombers such as the B-17 and Liberator. Geoffrey de Havilland's decision, in the summer of 1938, to go ahead with a twin-engined bomber principally of wooden construction, was vindicated during 1942-45 when the Mosquito bomber alone repeatedly won through against enemy defences to successfully attack targets.

The de Havilland Mosquito owed its lineage to the highly successful de Havilland Albatross airliner, capable, in the late 1930s of cruising at 210 mph (338 km/h) at 11,000 ft (3,353 m). Towards the end of 1938, Sir Wilfred Freeman, then member for Research, Development and Production on the Air Council, encouraged de Havilland to explore the possible military potential of a lightweight, streamlined bomber. In October 1938, Geoffrey de Havilland's design team, which included R.E. Bishop as chief designer and C.C. Walker as chief

Above right *The de Havilland Sea Mosquito TR 33 fitted with four-blade airscrews was used in small numbers by the Royal Navy as a carrier-borne or land-based strike aircraft armed with rocket projectiles and an 18 in torpedo or 2,000 lb (909 kg) of bombs (Hawker Siddeley).*

Right *Mosquito B XVI ML963 of No 571 Squadron (de Havilland).*

engineer, formulated a wooden monoplane design with two Merlin engines. Although the decision to use wood in the construction owed much to the company's long standing experience in wood working methods, the design team was aware of the imminent threat of war and the shortage of metals available to the aircraft industry.

By the time war had been declared in September 1939, de Havilland had come down in favour of a two-man, twin-engined, unarmed monoplane bomber. On 29 December 1939, the project received official backing when the Air Ministry asked for a basic requirement for a bomber capable of carrying a 1,000 lb (454 kg) bomb load with a range of 1,500 miles (2,415 km). On 1 March 1940, de Havilland received an order for just 50 aircraft against specification BI/40. This was in jeopardy following the Dunkirk débâcle of May 1940 when fears that Britain could be overrun prompted the Ministry of Aircraft Production to concentrate on established aircraft. For a time the 'wooden wonder', or DH 98 as it was known at de Havilland, was deleted from the priority list altogether. The fact that wood made up most of its construction worked in its favour and the type was soon reinstated.

Work began on three prototypes. The first was completed in just under 11 months since the beginning of detailed design and Captain de Havilland took the first prototype aloft on 25 November 1940 from Hatfield. Powered by two Merlin 21s, the new aircraft quickly showed its true potential, reaching a top speed of some 400 mph (644 km/h) and impressing officials with an outstanding display of manoeuvrability. Trials in February 1941 confirmed de Havilland's faith in the design but the Air Ministry favoured the fighter version. The contract for 50 bombers was pared down to just 20 bombers and the remainder fighters.

By July, the Mosquito was in full scale production but the requirement for the Mark IV bomber version (even the Mosquito trainer was ahead with the designation Mk III) was now down to just 10 (the other 10 being replaced

Mosquito B Mk IV of No 105 Squadron in 1943. This was the first RAF squadron to equip with the Mosquito and their first raid took place on 31 May 1942 during 'Operation Millenium' (Flt Lt Haywood).

with a requirement for the photo-reconnaissance version). The Mark IV Series I did not become operational. The Mark IV Series II differed principally from its predecessor in having lengthened engine nacelles and a larger bomb bay to increase tonnage to four 500 lb bombs instead of the Series I's four 250 pounders. In all, 263 Mosquito IVs were built, including 56 which were converted to carry a 4,000 lb 'Cookie' bomb. Thirty-two Mk IVs were later converted to PR IV reconnaissance aircraft.

The Mosquito IV began replacing the Blenheims of No. 2 (Light Bomber) Group of the RAF in the spring of 1942. No 105 Squadron at Swanton Morley were the first recipients, when Geoffrey de Havilland delivered 'Mk IV bomber conversion type' W4064 to the squadron on 15 November 1941. Four Mosquitoes belonging to this squadron made the first ever Mosquito bombing operation, at dawn on 31 May 1942, with a daylight raid on Cologne only a few hours after the 1,000 bomber raid on the city.

On 15 August 1942, No 8 Group (PFF) was formed and the pathfinder Mosquito, a modified Mk IV with special radar, entered service. On 25 September 1942, Mosquitoes of No 105 Squadron, Bomber Command, attacked the Gestapo Headquarters at Oslo in a daring rooftop attack in broad daylight. The flight to the target and back was made at sea level using dead reckoning all the way.

On the morning of 31 January 1943, the first Mosquitoes to bomb Berlin were those of No 105 Squadron when the attack was timed (incorrectly as it turned out) to break up a parade addressed by Herman Göring. Mosquitoes of No 139 Squadron returned in the afternoon to wreck another parade due to be inspected by the Reichsmarschall.

From May 1943 Mosquitoes of No 2 Group were taken off daylight operations as American 8th Air Force daylight missions gained momentum and many Mosquitoes were switched to Pathfinder operations underway with No 8 Group. Group Captain Leonard Cheshire received the Victoria Cross for the raid on Munich on the night of 24 April 1944, when he led four Mosquitos to mark the target with flares. Cheshire flew over the city at only 1,000 ft (804,9 m) during the early stages of the raid when bombs were falling. He continued to direct operations despite damage to his Mosquito, and only made for home after his mission had been accomplished. At this height his aircraft was the most vulnerable aircraft in the entire bomber stream.

On 23/24 February 1944, Mosquito BIVs of No 692 Squadron dropped 4,000 lb bombs for the first time, during a raid on Düsseldorf. During attacks on VI flying-bomb sites in Northern France in the summer of 1944 Mosquito squadrons averaged one Crossbow site destroyed for each 39.8 ton of bombs dropped compared with an average of about 200 ton for the Marauder and Mitchell combined. Eventually, 11 squadrons in No. 8 Group were equipped with the Mosquito and they were employed on all manner of operations, including nuisance raiding as part of what became known as the Light Night Striking Force. The Mk XVI was developed especially for this type of operation, differing mainly from the Mk IX in having a pressurized cabin which enabled it to operate as high as 40,000 ft (12,195 m). Light Night Striking Force Mosquitoes had the

lowest losses in Bomber Command (one per 2,000 sorties). From 20/21 February 1945 until 27/28 March, Bomber Command Mosquitoes made 36 consecutive night raids on Berlin.

On 12 March 1945 the Mosquito B Mk 35 flew for the first time. The B Mk 35 was powered by the Merlin 113-114 engine and had a maximum speed of 422 mph (679 km/h) at 30,000 ft (9,146 m). It had a service ceiling of 34,000 ft (10,365 m) and could carry a 4,000 lb bomb 1,750 miles (2,818 km) at 310 mph (499 km/h) at 30,000 ft (9,146 m). The B Mk 35 did not see operational service before the war ended.

No 8 Group Mossies had the honour of flying the last Bomber Command raid of the war, with an attack on Keil on 2 May 1945. The Mosquito equipped some 17 bomber squadrons in the Second World War and remained the fastest aircraft in service with Bomber Command until the end of the war. It was only eclipsed by the introduction of the Canberra jet bomber in 1951.

DORNIER DO 17/215

Type: *Medium bomber;* **Crew:** *Three;* **Manufacturers:** *Dornier-Werke G.mbH;* **Powerplant:** *(Do 17E-1) Two BMW VI radials;* **Dimensions:** *Span, 59 ft ½ in (18 m); Length, 53 ft 3¾ in (16.25 m); Height, 14 ft 2 in (4.3 m);* **Weight:** *Empty, 9,921 lb (4,500 kg); Loaded, 15,520 lb (7,050 kg);* **Performance:** *Max speed, 220 mph (355 km/h); Ceiling, 16,730 ft (5,100 m); Range, 620 miles (1,000 km);* **Armament:** *One 7.9 mm MG 15 firing aft from rear ventral hatch and one dorsal 7.9 mm MG 15. Bomb load, 1,650 lb (750 kg).*

The Dornier Do 17V-1 first emerged in 1934 as a result of a requirement issued by Lufthansa in 1933 for a high-speed mail and passenger airliner. In 1935, after evaluating three prototypes, Lufthansa decided against using the sleek monoplane because of the narrow confines available for the six passengers it was required to carry. All was not lost, however, and the type was converted to carry bombs.

Left *Dornier Do 17S-1 (Heinz J. Nowarra).*

Below *Dornier Do 17E-1s of KG 255 during military exercises in 1937 (Heinz J. Nowarra).*

Right *Two Dornier Do 17Zs in flight (Dornier GmbH).*

Dornier Do 17Z-2 (Heinz J. Nowarra).

During 1935, armed versions of the Do 17V-4-V-7 were flight tested, culminating in the Do 17E-1 first production model. In the spring of 1937, Do 17E-1 bombers and Do 17F-1 reconnaissance aircraft were deployed with the Legion Kondor fighting in the Spanish Civil War. In July the eighth prototype, the Do 17V-8 out-performed fighters of all other nations in the International Military Aircraft Competition in Switzerland. The Do 17V-8 became the Do 17M V-1, nicknamed the 'Flying Pencil' because of its graceful lines.

Experience in Spain revealed a need for nose defensive armament and better all-round vision for the pilot. This resulted in the Do 17S-01, which was powered by two Daimler Benz DB 600G liquid cooled radial engines. The final production model was the Do 17Z-0 which was introduced in 1938. Its two 900 hp Bramo 323A-1 radials gave insufficient power and the bomb load was limited to only 1,102 lb (500 kg). These faults were rectified in the Do 17Z-2, which flew in early 1939 powered by two 1,000 hp Bramo Fafnir 323P radials. With a crew of five it carried a bomb load of 2,205 lb (1,002 kg) and up to eight machine-guns.

Almost 1,700 Dornier Do 17s were produced before production ceased in July 1940 and well over 500 were used successfully during the blitzkrieg campaign, taking part in the bombing of Poland, the Low Countries and France. In the Battle of Britain the Do 17s, like all German bombers, suffered at the hands of RAF fighter pilots and were switched to bombing by night. On 7 September 1940, Do 17Zs were among over 600 aircraft which bombed London. On 6 April 1941, four Gruppen of Do 17Zs took part in the invasion of Greece and Yugoslavia. In July they were used in Operation 'Barborossa', the invasion of Russia.

Re-equipment with the Do 215B export version (to Sweden and Yugoslavia) of the Do 17 followed. About 100 Do 215B-0 bombers and B-1 reconnaissance versions were supplied to the Luftwaffe before production ceased in January 1941. In the spring of 1941 the Do 215B-5 night-fighter/intruder version model was issued to 4/NJG 2 for intruder operations

Dornier Do 215B-1 (Heinz J. Nowarra).

over the UK. It was fitted with a solid nose containing two 20 mm cannon and four 7.9 mm MG machine-guns. In 1942, all surviving Do 215s were replaced with the Junkers Ju 88 and Do 217.

DOUGLAS DB-7 (A-20) BOSTON

Type: *Light Day Bomber;* **Crew:** *Three;* **Manufacturers:** *Douglas Aircraft Co Inc, Santa Monica and Long Beach, California. Sub-Contracted by Boeing;* **Powerplant:** *Two GR-2600-A5B, -11, -23 or -29 Wright Double Cyclone radial engines;* **Dimensions:** *Span, 61 ft 4 in (18.69 m); Length, 48 ft 4 in (14.74 m); Height, 17 ft 7 in (5.36 m);* **Weight:** *Empty, 12,950 lb (5,874 kg); Loaded, 27,200 lb (12,340 kg);* **Performance:** *Max speed, 342 mph (549 km/h); Range, 1,000 miles (1,610 km); Service ceiling, 25,300 ft (7,720 m);* **Armament:** *(A-20G) Four 20 mm Hispano cannon and two .5 in/six .5 in in nose, dorsal turret with two .5 in and one hand-operated .5 in gun in ventral positions. Maximum bomb load, 4,000 lb (1,814 kg).*

Originally designed in 1938 as an attack bomber, the Douglas A-20 ranks among the most famous of its type during the Second World War. Its design was actually started in 1936 by Jack Northrop before his company was acquired by the Douglas Corporation. Ed Heinemann's design team improved the breed, adding the first tricycle nosewheel gear on an American military aircraft and more powerful Twin Wasps. The Model 7B, as it was re-designated, was entered for the July 1938 attack-bomber design competition, and the prototype flew on 26 October 1938.

On 15 February 1939 France ordered 100 DB-7 production aircraft, the first of which flew on 17 August that year. Sixty-four aircraft reached the Armée de l'Air, entering combat on 31 May 1940, and seeing limited action before the French surrender forced the surviving aircraft to relocate to North Africa. On 25 June, Britain took over all French contracts and undelivered aircraft, which included a contract for 170 DB-7s ordered by France in October 1939.

In RAF service all 15 Boston Is were used as

trainers, while about 200 Boston IIs (DB-7 and DB-7As) were converted to Havoc Is for night-fighting and night intruder operations. On 20 February 1940 Britain placed an order for the DB-7B version (similar to the US Army A-20A version but with .303 in guns in place of the .30 calibre models and Wright R-2600-A5B Cyclones instead of the R-2600-3s).

The DB-7B was known in RAF service as the Boston III and first entered service with No 88 Squadron at Swanton Morley, Norfolk, in October 1941 where it replaced the Blenheim IV. By December that year Douglas had delivered 541 examples, and a further 240 Boeing built DB-7Bs were delivered to Britain by January 1942. No 2 Group operated large numbers of Bostons on anti-shipping strikes and daylight raids against continental land targets. One of the most memorable Boston raids occurred on 8 March 1942 when the Matford Works at Poissy was attacked after an extremely low-level flight to confuse enemy radar.

Meanwhile, early in 1939 the Army Air Force had ordered 143 A-20As, and these were delivered to light bombardment groups in the USA and Hawaii. A simultaneous order for 63 A-20s which were to be fitted with R-2600-7 turbo-supercharged engines were not proceeded with, and all except one (which became the XP-70 night-fighter prototype) were used as photo-reconnaissance aircraft.

On 2 October the AAF ordered 999 A-20B models which benefited from recent combat experience. The A-20B was fitted with Wright R-2600-11 engines, self-sealing fuel tanks, armour plate, increased fuel tankage and .50 calibre guns in place of all but one of the earlier .30 calibres. Deliveries to the AAF commenced in December 1941. With American entry into the war, 162 Douglas-built and 194-Boeing built models for the RAF were diverted to the AAF, where the type was universally known as the Havoc after the British version. Six crews

Right *Douglas A-20A (Douglas).*

Below right *Douglas DB-7B in RAF markings (Douglas).*

Below *Boeing-built DB-7B AL 399, supplied to the RAF (Douglas).*

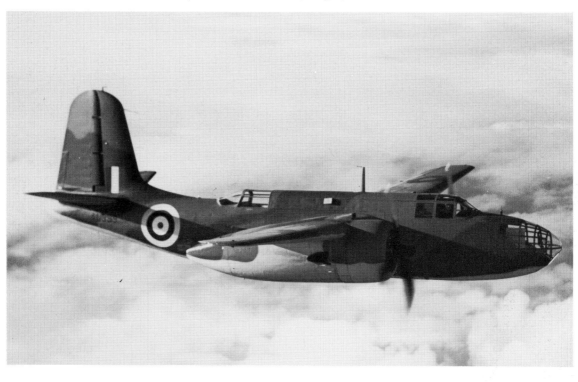

from the 15th Bomb Squadron and on 4 July 1942 six RAF crews, all flying DB-7Bs, carried out the first raid in which Americans participated on German airfields in Holland.

With war on other fronts taking precedence, some 151 Bostons were relinquished by the RAF for shipment to Russia. The Soviet Air Force received a total of 3,125 by the end of the war. Late in 1942 American deliveries to Britain were resumed, with 202 A-20C models supplied under lend-lease. This aircraft, similar to the DB-7B, was fitted with the R-2600-23 Cyclone and seven .30 calibre machine-guns. In RAF service the A-20C was known as the Boston IIIA. Altogether, about 980 Boston IIIs and IIIAs were delivered to the RAF.

In November 1942 the Boston entered service in North Africa, and in August 1943 UK-based Boston squadrons began operations with the newly created 2nd Tactical Air Force. The US 9th Air Force used the A-20 in tactical missions against German defences prior to the Normandy landings. On 6 June 1944 RAF Bostons laid smoke screens over the beaches and from the summer of that year the Boston IV, equipped with a power-operated dorsal turret, began operations with the RAF. Over 250 Boston IVs and Vs were transferred from the USAAF where they were designated A-20G and A-20J Havocs. These were attack bombers fitted with a solid 'gun nose' with awesome firepower supplied by 20 mm cannon and .50 calibre machine-guns. Boston IVs and Vs continued in service with the 2nd TAF in France and the Desert Air Force in Italy until VE Day.

In US service the 5th Air Force operated the A-20 at masthead height in the Pacific and used the aircraft to excellent effect during the battle for Dutch New Guinea, while the 47th Bomb Group of the 12th Air Force used it during the Italian campaign. When production of this magnificent aircraft ended in September 1944, 7,098 had been built by Douglas and 380 by Boeing.

Above right and right *Douglas Boston IIIs of No 114 Squadron, RAF, in North Africa* (Burberry).

ENGLISH ELECTRIC (BAC) CANBERRA

Type: *Light bomber;* **Crew:** *Three;* **Manufacturers:** *English Electric Aviation, Preston. Sub-Contracted by Avro, Handley Page and Short.;* **(B 2): Powerplant:** *Two Rolls-Royce Avon 101 turbojets;* **Dimensions:** *Span 63 ft 11½ in (19.5 m); Length, 65 ft 6 in (19.95 m). Height, 15 ft 7 in (4.72 m);* **Weight:** *Empty, 22,000 lb (10,000 kg); Loaded, 46,000 lb (20,909 kg);* **Performance:** *Max speed, 580 mph (933 km/h) at 30,000 ft (9,144 m); Ceiling, 48,000 ft (14,630 m); Range, 805 miles (1,295 km);* **Armament:** *None. Bomb load, 6,000 lb (2,727 kg).*

Designed by W.E.W. 'Teddy' Petter and known originally as the AI, the English Electric Canberra was the first jet bomber to enter service with the RAF. Because it was unarmed, the Canberra had to rely on speed alone to outpace interceptors. Specification B 3/45 called for a bomb load of 6,000 lb (2,727 kg) and a radius of action of 750 nautical miles. Petter designed an unswept aircraft with a broad, low-aspect ration wing which allowed for the highest possible cruising altitude and maximum fuel economy. It also bestowed remarkable manoeuvrability. Wing Commander Roland Beaumont demonstrated just how manoeuvrable the new aircraft was on 13 May 1949 when the prototype flew for the first time at Warton.

It was intended that the Canberra should have a crew of two and a radar bomb sight for bombing in all weathers, but a new specification, B 5/47, was introduced at the time of the fifth prototype for a crew of three and visual aiming in the nose. The first B 2, as the new type was designated, flew for the first time on 23 April 1950. The first production aircraft made its maiden flight on 8 October that year, and the first unit to be equipped was No 101 Squadron at Binbrook in May 1951.

Altogether, 430 Canberra B 2s were built. One set a transatlantic record in February 1951 when it was flown from the UK to Baltimore,

USA, as part of the deal which led to the Martin Company building the Canberra under licence (as the B 57/RB 57). This was a milestone in British aviation history. Not since the First World War had the USA built a foreign combat design in their own country.

The Korean war of 1950–53 caused a leap in demand for the Canberra and soon four factories were turning out B 2s. The PR 3 was a reconnaissance version with a longer fuselage to accommodate additional fuel tanks and the first entered service with No 540 Squadron at RAF Benson in 1953. The T 4 trainer followed and the Mk 5 prototype introduced Avon 109 engines and increased fuel tankage which were used on the B 6. This version began equipping RAF Bomber Command in June 1954. The PR 7 was a reconnaissance version of the B 6.

In February 1955 Canberra B 6s of No 101 Squadron became the first jet bombers in the Far East when they flew there as part of Operation 'Firedog', the emergency campaign against terrorists in Malaya. On 23 February, the first bombs were dropped in anger by RAF jet bombers when No 101 Squadron Canberras released them on the China Rock area during a 'Firedog' sortie.

The final Canberra bomber variant to serve with the RAF was the BI 8 two-seat light bomber/intruder which first entered service with No 88 Squadron in Germany in May 1956. The BI 8 differed from earlier Canberras in having a completely re-designed front fuselage with a blister-style canopy offset to port for the pilot and provision for a navigator/bomb aimer in the nose. A detachable gun pack capable of housing either four 20 mm or 30 mm cannon was mounted beneath the rear section of the bomb bay.

During October-November 1956 Canberra B 2s from Cyprus and B 6s from both Cyprus and Malta took part in operations against Egypt during the Suez Crisis. On 31 October, a Canberra B 2 of No 10 Squadron became the first RAF aircraft to drop bombs during the crisis.

Right *Canberra B1 8 WT329 (BAe).*
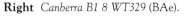

Canberra B 15 WT307 modified to B Mk 6 (BAe).

At home, Canberra light bombers were gradually phased out and formed a nuclear strike force in support of CENTO with the Near East Air Force in Cyprus and in the Far East. On 11 September 1961, the last Canberra squadron in Bomber Command disappeared from the inventory with the disbandment of No 35 Squadron at Upwood. During 1963, the Canberra BI 8 was modified to carry two Nord AS 30 air-to-surface missiles for conventional interdiction duties, day or night. The BI 8 continued in its primary low-level nuclear role in Germany until June 1972 when No 16 Squadron at Laarbruch disbanded.

Total Canberra production reached 925 in Britain and a further 49 B 20 versions were built in Australia for the RAAF. Today only No 100 Squadron of RAF Strike Command at Wyton use the Canberra B Mk 2, T Mk 4, E Mk 15 and TT Mk 18 for target facilities, towed for air and ground gunners 'silent' to test air and ground radar operators. The Canberra ranks as one of the most successful British designs of all time with export versions to about 10 different nations, where rebuilt versions still serve in some instances as tactical bombers.

GENERAL DYNAMICS FB-111A-F

Type: *Attack bomber;* **Crew:** *Two;* **Manufacturers:** *General Dynamics, Fort Worth, Texas;* **Powerplant:** *(FB-111) Two Pratt & Whitney TF30-7 turbofans.* **Dimensions:** *Span (extended), 70 ft (21.34 m); Length, 73 ft 6 in (22.4 m); Height, 17 ft 1½ in (5.22 m);* **Weight:** *Empty, 50,000 lb (22,680 kg); Loaded, 119,000 lb (54,000 kg);* **Performance:** *Max speed, Mach 2.2 (about 1,450 mph 2,335 km/h) at 35,000 ft (10,670 m);* **Armament:** *Internal weapons bay for two 750 lb (341 kg) bombs or 20 mm M-61 rotary cannon. Eight underwing pylons for 31,500 lb (14,290 kg) stores.*

The swing-wing F-111, which first flew on 21 December 1964, is still one of the most remarkable aircraft in the USAF inventory. However, its early career was extremely disappointing. Originally, the F-111A was designed to give Tactical Air Command an all-weather strike capability and deliveries to the USAF began in June 1967. Despite this, only 141 F-111As were built. Two production F-111Bs were delivered to the US Navy before this project was cut short. It was only after problems in range deficiency, structure and engine power were overcome that the F-111 grew in stature, although General Dynamics suffered another setback when an order from Britain for 50 models similar to the RAAF F-111C was later cancelled.

The F-111's wing sweep can be varied in flight to provide stable, efficient performance throughout flight from slow approach speeds to more than twice the speed of sound. Fully extended to 16° of sweep, the wing creates maximum span and surface area for maximum lift during short take-offs and landings. Another unique feature is the pilot's cockpit module, which in emergency is parted from the aircraft by an explosive cutting cord and ejected upward by a rocket motor, before the capsule descends by parachute to be used as a survival module on land or sea.

The FB-111 is a variation of the tactical fighter and has slightly longer wing tips. The FB-111A, which was fitted with two Pratt & Whitney TF30-P-7 engines, was developed to provide Strategic Air Command with a high-altitude/conventional bombing replacement for some of its B-52C and B-52F Stratofortresses and B-58A Hustlers. The first of 76 FB-111A production aircraft flew in July 1968. Deliveries to the 340th Bomb Wing began in October 1969.

The F-111E, of which 94 were built, was based on the F-111A basic design, but with improved

General Dynamics FB-111A 39783 tactical fighter-bomber of Strategic Air Command (General Dynamics).

penetration aids and weapons management system and inlet sized to accept improved versions of the TF30 engine. The F-111D, of which 96 were built, introduced a digital computer fire control/bombing system to provide air-to-ground, moving target capability plus improved navigation and weapons delivery accuracy. It also had the improved TF30-P-9 engines. The fifth and final F-111 for the USAF, the 'F' is fitted with two TF30-P-100 engines which gives dramatic improvement in performance, increased payload and greater manoeuvrability. Some 106 F-111Fs were built.

In addition to the models for the USAF, General Dynamics built 24 F-111Cs for the Royal Australian Air Force. The first F-111C flew in July 1968 and production models were delivered to the RAAF in 1973. The RAAF F-111C is similar to the F-111A, but it has the additional 7 ft (2.13 m) wingspan, the strengthened landing gear and larger tyres and brakes of the FB-111A.

The last of 562 F-111s (including 23 research and development aircraft, 18 for the USAF and five for the US Navy) rolled off the production line at General Dynamics plant at Fort Worth, Texas, in September 1976.

In SAC, a total of some 60 FB-111As equip the 380th Strategic Aerospace Wing at Platts-burgh AFB, New York and the 509th Bomb Wing at Pease AFB, New Hampshire. In Tactical Air Force the F-111A equips the 366th Tactical Fighter Wing at Mountain Home AFB, Idaho and the F-111D equips the 27th TFW at Cannon AFB, New Mexico.

Over 150 F-111Es and F-111Fs are based in England for NATO duty. The FB-111E serves with the 20th Tactical Fighter Wing at Upper Heyford and the 48th TFW is based at Lakenheath, equipped with the FB-111F. On 15 April 1986, FB-111s operating from these two British bases, together with Grumman-built EF-111A electronic suppression aircraft, took part in Operation 'El Dorado Canyon' which involved raids on targets in Libya. The aircraft were refuelled *en route* and returned over the Atlantic and the Mediterranean. One aircraft failed to return.

Updates will ensure that the FB-111 will continue in first-line service into the 1990s, when all FB-111s will be reassigned to Tactical Air Command pending the introduction of the Northrop ATB (Advanced Technology Bomber) to SAC.

An F-111F of the 48th TFW takes off on full power after an emergency stop over at RAF Coltishall on 14 May 1982.

Gotha G Vb (Heinz J. Nowarra).

GOTHA G IV/VB

Type: *Long-range bomber;* **Crew:** *Three;* **Manufacturers:** *Gothaer Waggonfabrik AG, Luft Verkehrs G.mbH, Siemens Schuckert Werke G.mbH;* **Powerplant:** *(G IV) Two 260 hp Mercedes DIVa pusher engines;* **Dimensions:** *Span, 77 ft 10 in (23.5 m); Length, 38 ft 11 in (11.61 m); Height, 14 ft 1 in (4.29 m);* **Weight:** *Empty, 5,280 lb (2,400 kg); Loaded, 7,997 lb (3,635 kg);* **Performance:** *Max speed, 90 mph (144.9 km/h); Ceiling; 21,320 ft (6,500 m) Range, 522 miles (840 km);* **Armament:** *Bomb load, 1,100 lb (500 kg).*

The idea of raiding south-east England with aeroplanes based at Calais was first considered by Major Wilhelm Siegert, commander of the Brieftauben-Abteilung Ostende (Carrier-Pigeon Flight, Ostend), in October 1914. However, the German Army was forced to retreat from the area and Siegert had to content himself with raids on French Channel ports. In April 1915, the Flight was withdrawn to Metz. There, crews waited until German designers could develop an aircraft of the size capable of long-range operation.

On 31 May 1915, Zeppelins made their first ever night bombing raid on London, forcing the RFC to divert many valuable aircraft from the Front to Home Defence. In 1915, with Germany anxious to maintain the ascendancy, 20 giant bombers from no less than six different manufacturers reached the German Military Aviation Service. In any event, no raids were made on England because of German reverses on the Western Front.

In 1916 General Ernst von Hoeppner took command of the Military Aviation Service, which was renamed 'Luftstreitkrafte'. Hoeppner proposed the formation of a squadron of 30 Gotha bombers which would bomb London from bases in Belgium. The G II, powered by two 220 hp Benz engines, entered service late in 1916 but was soon withdrawn owing to engine failures, and was replaced by the G III which was fitted with the more reliable D IVa powerplant. The G IV, of which 230 were built, entered service in March 1917 with 'Kampfgeschwader Nr 3' (the 'England squadron') for raids on England.

On 25 May 1917, 23 Gothas took off from Gontrode and St Denis-Westrem and after refuelling at Nieuwmunster near the Belgian coast, headed across the Channel for London. Two dropped out of formation and the remaining 21 reached Essex, only to be defeated by towering cloud banks near the capital. The formation turned south and released its bombs on targets of opportunity near Kent. The main bomb tonnage was released on Folkestone, killing or injuring 355 people. On 13 June, the first major Gotha raid on London resulted in 162 dead and 426 injured. Gotha daylight raids on southern England and London continued spasmodically until August 1917.

In August 1917 the G V entered service, but the British defences had become extremely effective and the decision was taken to despatch the bombers by night. The first night mission took place on 2/3 September 1917 and for nine months Gothas and later designs like the massive 'Riesenflugzeug' or 'Giant', sometimes joined by Zeppelins, made spasmodic raids on London and southern England. The raids caused great loss of life and political in-fighting in the Houses of Parliament. As a result the British night defences were strengthened and the German bases in Belgium were bombed constantly.

The last night raid on London took place on 19/20 May 1918, when six of the ten bombers that reached the capital were shot down by the home defences. It was the last aerial attack on the United Kingdom until German bombers returned in the Second World War.

Above *Gotha G IV* (Heinz J. Nowarra).

Below *Handley Page 0/400 C9700 at Provin, France whilst en route to Egypt in November 1918. This aircraft was wrecked in a cyclone at Lahore in April 1919* (Norfolk & Suffolk Aviation Museum).

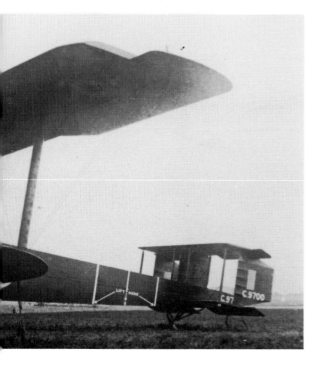

HANDLEY PAGE 0/100 AND 0/400

Type: *Long-range bomber;* **Crew:** *Four;* **Manufacturers:** *Handley Page Ltd, Cricklewood, London;* **Powerplant:** *(0/400) Two Rolls-Royce Eagle VIII engines;* **Dimensions:** *Span, 100 ft (30.48 m); Length, 62 ft 10¼ in (18.93 m); Height, 22 ft (6.7 m);* **Weight:** *Empty, about 8,000 lb (3,636 kg); Loaded, 13,360 lb (6,072 kg);* **Performance:** *Max speed, 97.5 mph (157 km/h);* **Armament:** *Bomb load, 1,792 lb (814.5 kg).*

During the first few months of the First World War Allied Commanders drew up plans for the formation of a strategic bombing unit for attacks on German targets such as Zeppelin sheds and supply depots far behind the enemy lines. At first, Sopwith 1½ Strutters and other types were used but without success, so in December 1914 the Admiralty Air Department issued a specification for a two-seat aircraft capable of carrying a minimum bomb load of six 100 lb bombs. Handley Page designed the 0/100 to meet the requirement and the type was flown for the first time on 18 December 1915. In its production form the 0/100 could carry 16 112 lb bombs and the crew was increased to four.

Deliveries to the RNAS began on 27 May 1916, to No 1456 Squadron. The first front-line unit to receive the 0/100 was the Fifth Naval Wing at Dunkirk in November 1916. By the end of 1917 the RNAS had four squadrons of 0/100s in its inventory and these units made many night raids on German aerodromes, U-boat bases and lines of communication. On 9 July 1917, one 0/100 bombed Constantinople and attacked the battle cruiser *Goeben* . Two 112 lb bombs were dropped on the Turkish War Office and eight on the *Goeben*. A total of 46 0/100s was built before production was switched to the 0/400.

The 0/400 had a completely revised fuel system and could easily be distinguished from the 0/100 by the removal of the fuel tanks from behind the engine nacelles. The 0/400 saw widespread operation with VIII Brigade (later

Handley Page Heyford Mk IAs of No 10 Squadron, July 1935. No 10 squadron received its first Heyford on 3 August 1934 and re-equipment was completed by mid-November that year (Flight).

Independent Force, RAF), bombing German cities by day and by night. By the end of the First World War, the 0/400 equipped eight RAF squadrons and about 400 had been delivered before the Armistice. The 0/400 could carry 16 112 lb bombs inside the fuselage or a single 1,650 lb bomb, the largest used by the RAF in the First World War. The bomb bay was covered by spring-loaded doors which opened under the weight of the bombs as they were released. Two additional bombs could be carried on external racks under the fuselage. In all, some 554 0/400s were built, including about 100 in the USA.

The 0/400 remained in service with the RAF for a short time after the war, before being replaced by the Vimy and the de Havilland Amiens. Some were converted to civilian airliners, although Nos 70 and 216 Squadrons operated the 0/400 in Egypt until 1920.

HANDLEY PAGE HEYFORD

Type: *Heavy Night bomber;* **Crew:** *Four;* **Manufacturers:** *Handley Page, Cricklewood, London;* **Powerplant:** *Two Rolls-Royce Kestrel IIIS or IIIS-5;* **Dimensions:** *Span, 75 ft (22.86 m); Length, 58 ft (17.68 m); Height, 17 ft 6 in (5.36 m);* **Weight:** *Empty, 9,200 lb (4,181 kg); Loaded, 16,900 lb (7,681 kg);* **Performance:** *Max speed, 142 mph (228.6 km/h) at 13,000 ft (3,963 m); Ceiling, 21,000 ft (6,402 m); Range, 920 miles (1,481 km);* **Armament:** *Bomb load (maximum), 3,500 lb (1,590 kg).*

The Heyford was the last of the biplane heavy bombers to see service with the RAF and was unusual in that its fuselage was attached to the upper wing instead of the lower. The bomb load was concentrated in the thickened centre section of the lower wing which permitted short re-loading times.

The prototype HP 38, built to Specification B 19/27, flew for the first time in June 1930 at Radlett. It was powered by two Kestrel II engines and was of fabric-covered, all-metal construction. The Heyford Mk I production

model, which first flew on 21 June 1933, differed from the prototype in having Kestrel III engines and a partly aluminium-covered fuselage. The first Mk Is began equipping 99 Squadron at Upper Heyford in July 1933.

Eventually, the type equipped 11 RAF squadrons and when production ceased in July 1936, a total of 124 had been delivered. In 1937, the Heyford was joined in RAF service by the new breed of monoplane bombers which included the Whitley and Wellesley. Gradually all remaining Heyfords were replaced entirely by the Wellington in 1939.

HANDLEY PAGE HALIFAX I~VII

Type: *Heavy bomber;* **Crew:** *Seven;* **Manufacturers:** *Handley Page Ltd, Cricklewood, London. Mk VI also built by English Electric;* **Powerplant:** *(Mk I) Four Rolls-Royce Merlin X. (Mk VI) Four Bristol Hercules 100;* **Dimensions:** *(VI) Span, 104 ft 2 in (31.75 m); Length, 71 ft 7 in (21.82 m); Height, 20 ft 9 in (6.32 m);* **Weight:** *Empty, 39,000 lb (17,690 kg); Loaded, 68,000 lb (30,844 kg);* **Performance:** *Max speed, 312 mph (501 km/h) at 22,000 ft (6,707 m); Range, 1,260 miles (2,030 km); Ceiling, 24,000 ft (7,315 m);* **Armament:** *One .303 in machine-gun in nose and two power-operated turrets each containing four .303 in guns. Bomb load, 13,000 lb (5,909 kg).*

The Halifax was designed to the same specification, P 13/36, which led to the ill-fated Avro Manchester. The requirement was for an all-metal, mid-wing, medium-heavy bomber powered by the same twin Rolls-Royce Vulture engine which was to cause the downfall of the Manchester.

Luckily for the Halifax an anticipated shortage of Vultures led to the original design being revised to take four Merlin engines. The production specification, 32.37, was written round the revised design. This resulted in an overall increase in dimensions and all-up weight from 26,300 lb (11,954 kg) on the original Handley Page HP 56 design to 40,000 lb (18,181 kg) on the new four-engined version which was designated the HP 57. The prototype bomber, now

called the Halifax, flew for the first time on 25 October 1939 at Bicester.

Initially, 100 Halifaxes were ordered by the Air Ministry but this was later increased in line with an Air Staff heavy bomber programme which anticipated 500 Halifaxes in service by April 1942, together with 1,500 Stirlings and 1,500 Manchesters. However, it was with the Lancaster that the Halifax was to share the major part of the RAF offensive against Germany. The Lancaster was more famous than the Halifax, but it served throughout the war solely as a bomber, while the Halifax was employed in several roles, including transport, general reconnaissance and anti submarine operations with Coastal Command.

The Halifax, together with the Wellington and the Stirling, took the leading role in the early heavy bomber raids on enemy territory, until the Lancaster was available in large numbers. The Halifax Mk I began equipping No 35 Squadron at Boscombe Down in November 1940 and made its first operational sortie on

Halifax B II Series I W7676 of No 35 (Madras Presidency) Squadron. This aircraft was lost on the night of 28/29 August 1942 during a raid on Nuremberg (via Mike Bailey).

the night of 10/11 March 1941 with a raid on Le Havre. The next night, the Halifax became the first RAF four-engined bomber (with the Manchester) to drop bombs on Germany, during a raid on Hamburg.

In July 1941, 'Halibags', as they were nicknamed, temporarily abandoned their nocturnal role and made an outstanding attack on the *Scharnhorst* docked at La Pallice. Halifaxes reverted to their night offensive at the end of 1941 after further attacks on German capital ships. On the night of 10/11 April 1942, an 8,000 lb bomb was first used operationally when one was dropped on Essen by a Halifax II of No 76 Squadron.

Between 1941 and 1945 they flew 75,532 sorties and dropped 227,610 tons of bombs compared to the Lancaster's 156,000 sorties and

608,612 tons of bombs. Some 2,050 Halifax I and II models were built. At the end of 1942, the Halifax II Series IA entered service with Coastal Command and were designated GR II Series I and IA. Some were fitted with four-blade airscrews and all had a .5 in machine-gun in the nose. The GR II was followed by a maritime version of the Halifax V which served with Coastal Command on both ASW and meteorological reconnaissance duties from bases in Britain and Gibraltar.

Some 2,081 Mk III models were built and were followed by 916 Mk V (General Duties) versions and 557 Mk VIs. A total of 193 Mk VII models were completed and a total of 96 Halifax C VIIIs were built shortly before the end of the Second World War. These were used as troop carriers and supply droppers for the airborne forces until superseded in 1946 by the Hastings. Many C VIIIs were later converted to Haltons for use with commercial companies.

A further 674 Halifaxes of varying marks, the last of which was the A IX (which was the final type, delivered in November 1946), saw service with the RAF in Palestine and India until September 1946 and December 1947 respectively. A total of 6,176 Halifaxes had been built when production ceased on 20 November 1946. On 17 March 1952 the last Halifax in first-line service with the RAF, a GR 6 of No 224 Squadron, made its final sortie.

HANDLEY PAGE VICTOR

Type: *Medium bomber (later tanker);* **Crew:** *Five;* **Manufacturers:** *Handley Page Ltd, Cricklewood, London;* **Powerplant:** *(B 2) Four Rolls-Royce Conway R Co 17 Mk 201 turbofans;* **Dimensions:** *Span, 120 ft (36.58 m); Length, 114 ft 11 in (35.05 m); Height, 30 ft 1½ in (9.2 m);* **Weight:** *Empty, 91,000 lb (41,277 kg); Loaded, 233,000 lb (101,150 kg);* **Performance:** *Max speed, Mach 0.92 (640 mph 1,030 km/h) at 40,000 ft (12,195 m); Range, 4,600 miles (7,400 km); Ceiling, 60,000 ft (18,290 m);* **Armament:** *None. Bomb load, 35 1,000 lb bombs or nuclear bombload and provision for one Blue Steel "stand-off" bomb.*

Designed to meet the same Air Ministry specification as the Vulcan (B 35/46), the crescent-wing Victor was the third and final V-bomber (the Valiant was the first) to be built for the RAF. The prototype Victor flew for the first time on Christmas Eve, 1952. At this time it was generally accepted that current high speed, high altitude jet bombers could outfly interceptors of the day. However, its development was so protracted that by the time it entered operational service with the RAF with No 10 Squadron at Cottesmore in April 1958, it was no longer immune to fighters and missiles.

The Victor B 1 was superseded by the Victor B 2 in first-line service. starting with No 159

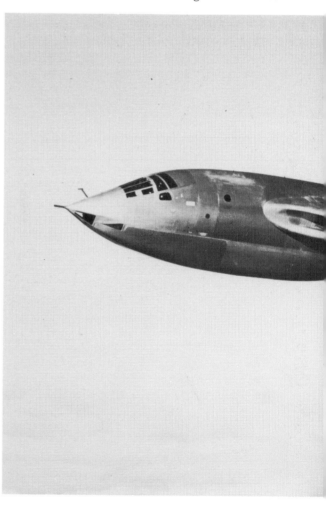

Right *Victor K Mk 2 of No 55 Squadron deploys its brake 'chute during landing at RAF Marham in September 1986.*

Below *First production Victor B 1 XA917 which first flew on 1 February 1956 (BAe).*

Squadron at Wittering in February 1962. The B 2 was a development of the Mk I and Mk IA, powered by four 20,600 lb thrust Rolls-Royce Conway RCo 17 Mk 201 engines. It differed externally from the B 1 in having wings of greater span, enlarged air intakes, a dorsal fillet forward of the fin and two retractable scoops near the tail to supply ram air to two turbo-alternators for emergency power supplies. Like the Vulcan B 2, the Victor B 2 BS could carry the Blue Steel stand-off bomb. In January 1964, Victors and Vulcans were switched to the low-level role with conventional gravity bombs or a nuclear payload. The Victor SR 2 was the strategic reconnaissance version and first entered service with No 543 Squadron at Wyton in late 1965. SR 2s differed from previous versions in having a bomb bay converted to accommodate camera equipment and additional fuel tanks for increased range.

During 1965–67 all Victors were converted to K IA air-to-air refuellers in the air tanker role, and were equipped with up to three refuelling points for fuel transfer. By the end of 1968, both Nos 100 and 139 Squadrons had been disbanded and 16 of their aircraft were subsequently modified to Victor K 2 standard, replacing the K I tankers at Marham, Norfolk.

The SR 2s of 543 Squadron continued in service until May 1974 when the Squadron disbanded. A total of 24 K 2 tankers equipped Nos 55 and 57 Squadrons at RAF Marham until No 57 Squadron disbanded on 30 June 1986, leaving No 55 Squadron as the sole operator of the Victor.

HAWKER HART

Type: *Light day-bomber;* **Crew:** *Two;* **Manufacturers:** *Hawker Aircraft Co, Kingston, Surrey. Subcontracted by Armstrong Whitworth, Gloster and Vickers;* **Powerplant:** *One Rolls-Royce Kestrel IB or Kestrel X (DR);* **Dimensions:** *Span, 37 ft 3 in (11.37 m); Length, 29 ft 4 in (8.96 m); Height, 10 ft 5 in (3.2 m);* **Weights:** *Empty, 2,530 lb (1,150 kg); Loaded, 4,554 lb (2,070 kg);* **Performance:** *Max speed, 184 mph (296 km/h); Range, 470 miles (756 km); Ceiling, 21,320 ft (6,500 m);* **Armament:** *One Vickers gun firing forward, one Lewis gun firing aft. Bomb load, 500 lb (227 kg).*

Facing page *Hawker Hart J9941, one of 15 development aircraft built and which, despite the No 57 (for 57 Squadron), saw service with No 33 Squadron in 1930 (BAe and Hawker Siddeley).*

Below *Hawker Hart Is of No 33 Squadron probably taken at Ramleh, Palestine during the summer of 1936. The nearest three aircraft are (left to right) K4456, K4449 and K4448 (Norfolk and Suffolk Aviation Museum).*

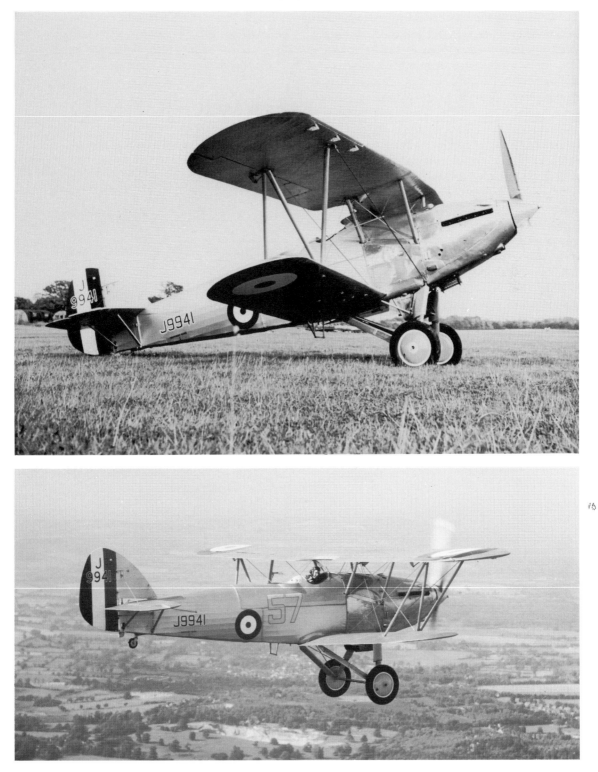

This, the most famous British military biplane between the wars, was built in larger numbers than any other basic design. It was accepted by the Air Ministry after competitive trials with the Fairey Fox II and the Avro Antelope, and initial production of 15 development aircraft were issued to No 33 Squadron at Eastchurch in January 1930, where they replaced the Hawker Horsley. The Hart was very manoeuvrable for its day and during the 1930 Air Exercises it caused a few red faces among officers of the Air Staff by outpacing Siskin fighters.

Between 1930 and 1936, Harts equipped some seven bomber squadrons and eight AAF Squadrons. Overseas, Harts served in Egypt and Palestine and from November 1931 in India where they began replacing the Westland Wapiti. Harts continued to serve with home-based light bomber squadrons until 1936 when they were replaced by the Hawker Hind and in India until 1939 when they gave way to the Bristol Blenheim.

A total of about 460 Harts was built and sub-variants included the Hart (C) for Communications duties, Hart (India) and the Hart (Special). The Special was an Audax airframe modified to carry desert equipment and was fitted with a tropical radiator, a braked undercarriage with heavy-duty tyres and a de-rated Rolls-Royce Kestrel X engine.

HAWKER HIND

Type: *Light bomber;* **Crew:** *Two;* **Manufacturers:** *Hawker Aircraft Co, Kingston, Surrey;* **Powerplant:** *One Rolls-Royce Kestrel V;* **Dimensions:** *Span, 37 ft 3 in (11.35 m); Length, 29 ft 7 in (9.02 m); Height, 10 ft 7 in (3.23 m);* **Weight:** *Empty, 3,251 lb (1,475 kg); Loaded, 5,298 lb (2,403 kg);* **Performance:** *Max speed, 186 mph (299 km/h) at 16,400 ft (4,999 m); Range, 430 miles (692 km); Service ceiling, 26,400 ft (8,047 m);* **Armament:** *One Vickers gun firing forward, one Lewis gun firing aft. Bomb load, 500 lb (227 kg).*

One of the most successful Hart derivatives, the Hind equipped some 20 light bomber squadrons of the RAF during 1935~39. It was most important in that it permitted the formation of many bomber squadrons during the RAF Expansion period in preparation for the

Hawker Hind K6689 (Hawker Siddeley Aviation).

deliveries of more advanced aircraft like the Blenheim, Battle and Wellington.

The Hind differed from the Hart in having a fully-supercharged Kestrel V engine, a tail-wheel in place of the skid, and a cut-away gunner's cockpit similar to the Demon. Production models were characterized by ram's horn exhaust manifolds. The prototype Hind made its maiden flight at Brooklands on 12 September 1934, and production models began equipping No 21 Squadron at Bircham Newton, Norfolk, in December 1935.

When production ceased in September 1938 a total of 528 Hinds, including trainers, had been delivered to the RAF. Small numbers of export versions were sold to several foreign air forces including Afghanistan (which took delivery of eight followed by 12 ex-RAF models), Persia, Portugal and Switzerland (which ordered one). An ex-seaplane version was later sold to the Yugoslavian Air Force, and in 1939-40 Eire purchased six ex-RAF Hinds.

The Hind was finally replaced in first-line service in June 1939, although the type rendered useful service with the RAF for a short time after that.

HEINKEL HE 111

Type: *Medium bomber;* **Crew:** *Four-five;* **Manufacturers:** *Ernst Heinkel AG; also built by SNCASO, France and under licence by Fabrica de Avione SET, Romania and CASA, Spain;* **Powerplant:** *(111H-6) Two Junkers Jumo 211F-2;* **Dimensions:** *Span, 74 ft 1¾ in (22.6 m); Length, 53 ft 9½ in) (16.4 m); Height, 13 ft 1½ in (4 m);* **Weight:** *Empty, 17,000 lb (7,720 kg); Loaded, 30,865 lb (14,000 kg);* **Performance:** *Max speed, 258 mph (415 km/h) at 16,400 ft (5,000 m); Ceiling, 25,590 ft (7,800 m); Max range, 745 miles (1,200 km);* **Armament:** *Five 7.9 mm machine-guns, one forward firing 20 mm MG FF cannon, one MG 17 machine-gun. Bomb load (maximum) 5,510 lb (2,505 kg) or two torpedoes.*

Design work on the new high-speed monoplane bomber and transport for the Luftwaffe was begun in 1934. The elliptical winged, all-metal Heinkel 111 owed much to the four passenger high speed Heinkel He 70 transport. To cover its true purpose the He 111a prototype, which flew for the first time on 24 February 1935, was unveiled as a civil airliner.

Heinkel He 111H-2s of 7/KG 1 in August 1940 (Hans Heiri Stapfer).

On 12 March 1935, the He 111 V2 transport version flew for the first time. Camouflaged in the livery of Deutsche Lufthansa it made several clandestine reconnaissance flights over the USSR, England and France. The He 111 V3 bomber version became the forerunner of the He 111A production model. The early He 111A proved unsuitable for military use, being too heavy and slow when loaded with military equipment.

The He 111B-1, which made its maiden flight on 30 October 1936, fared a little better. Powered by 880 hp DB 600C engines the He 111B-1 carried an armament of three 7.9 mm MG 15 machine-guns in the nose and ventral positions. Delivery to the Luftwaffe was begun that year and in February 1937 the type equipped the Legion Kondor in Spain. The Republican fighters were easily outpaced by the sleek new bomber and it proved very successful on bombing operations. A few He 111D-0s were built late in 1937 before production was given over to the He 111E model. Approximately 200 He 111Es were built.

The He 111P-1, which featured the familar glazed aerodynamic nose, entered service with the Luftwaffe in the spring of 1939. Only a few Ps were built before production switched to the He 111H, which was powered by two Junkers Jumo 211 engines. The He 111 were used in large numbers during the opening onslaught against Poland in September 1939 with great success. During the winter of 1939-40 Heinkel Hs and Ps were used in anti-shipping strikes and they took part in the invasion of Norway and Denmark in early April 1940. About 100 He 111Ps were used to flatten the Dutch capital, Rotterdam, on 14 May 1940.

By the time of the Battle of Britain, many He 111 units had been re-equipped with the Ju 88 but those that remained were badly mauled in daylight raids over England. Heinkels were switched to the night bombing of London and other English towns. Fitted with the Knickebein radio navigational aid, He 111s of KGr 100 were particularly successful in raids on the Spitfire factory at Castle Bromwich on the night of 13 August 1940 and Coventry on the night of 14 November 1940.

Heinkel 111s were used in small numbers in the Mediterranean and in May-June 1941 five Geschwader operated the type in Russia. One of the He 111's last major successes was on the night of 21/22 June 1944 when 43 B-17s and 15 Mustangs were destroyed by their bombs at Poltava, Russia.

Over 6,000 He 111s were built in Germany and Romania and this figure includes many sub-types like the He 111H-6 torpedo bomber and the five engined He 111Z-1 (two He 111H-6 airframes joined together). Post-war, Spanish built C.2111 versions with Merlin engines continued to be produced until 1956.

JUNKERS JU 87 STUKA

Type: *Dive bomber;* **Crew:** *Two;* **Manufacturers:** *Junkers Flugzeug und Motorenwerke AG. Also built by Weser Flugzeugbau and SNCASO, France;* **Powerplant:** *(Ju 87D-1) One Junkers Jumo 211J-1;* **Dimensions:** *Span, 45 ft 3¼ in (13.8 m); Length, 36 ft 5 in (11.1 m); Height, 12 ft 9 in (3.9 m);* **Weight:** *Empty, 6,080 lb (2,750 kg); Loaded, 12,600 lb (5,720 kg);* **Performance:** *Max speed, 255 mph (408 km/h) at 13,500 ft (4,115 m); Ceiling, 24,000 ft (7,320 m); Range, 620 miles (1,000 km);* **Armament:** *Two wing-mounted 7.9 mm MG 17 machine-guns and two 7.9 mm MG 81 machine-guns in rear cockpit. One 1,102 lb (500 kg) bomb under fuselage and four 110 lb (50 kg) underwing bombs*

On 27 September 1933, Germany placed a contract for the design of a Sturzkampffugzeug, or dive-bomber. Four designs were submitted and the Ju 87 VI emerged victorious. The twin-finned prototype made its maiden flight in the late spring of 1935, being powered by a Rolls-Royce Kestrel V engine. In 1936, the Ju 87 was

Top left *Heinkel He 111H-6 (Heinz J. Nowarra).*

Centre left *Heinkel He 111E-3 of KG 1* Hindenburg *(Heinz J. Nowarra).*

Left *CASA 2111 BR-2-I-129 of the Spanish Air Force pictured at the Paris Air Show on 10 June 1979 (Harry Holmes).*

Above *Junkers Ju 87B (Heinz J. Nowarra).*

transferred to a new Luftwaffe Research centre at Rechlin for final evaluation.

In 1937, the Ju 87A, with wide trouser undercarriage fairings, entered production. The Ju 87B had a completely redesigned cockpit canopy, enlarged vertical tail surfaces and spatted undercarriage. An additional MG 17 machine-gun was installed in the port wing. In December 1940, three Ju 87As which had been sent to join the Legion Kondor in Spain made their bombing début with a raid on Teruel. The dive-bomber proved so successful that more Ju 87As were despatched, and late in 1938 the first Ju 87Bs began arriving in Spain.

Evaluation under combat conditions greatly aided Stuka development. The Ju 87D, which appeared in the spring of 1940, was fitted with the more powerful 1,400 hp Junkers Jumo 211J engine and the oil cooler was moved from on top of the engine to below it, while the oil coolant radiator was re-sited below the wings. More armour was added and the MG 15 machine-gun in the cockpit was replaced by a

Above *Junkers Ju 87D-1* (Heinz J. Nowarra).

Left *Junkers Ju 87B of the Royal Hungarian Air Force. Hungarian Stukas took part in several attacks on the Eastern Front during the Second World War* (Hans Heiri Stapfer).

twin MG 81Z to provide greater firepower.

The morale-sapping effect of a siren mounted beneath the fuselage first used during dive bombing in Spain was not lost on the Luftwaffe, which used it to even greater effect during the bombing of Poland, Norway and Denmark, France and the Low Countries in 1939–40. Luftwaffe superiority was total and Stuka losses were negligible. It was a rude shock, therefore, when Stuka crews had no answer to severe losses caused by RAF Spitfires and Hurricanes over France during the evacuation of the BEF from Dunkirk. The Stuka's invincibility was shattered in the Battle of Britain. During the first two weeks of August 1940 the eight Stuka Gruppen lost 39 of its 281 Stukas, with 17 being lost on 18 August alone. Another 12 aircraft were shot down the following day during a raid on a radar station, and the

Ju 87 was withdrawn from the Battle.

Early in January 1941, many Stukas were transferred to Sicily where for a short time they enjoyed successful strikes on Allied shipping in the Mediterranean. Further Stuka Gruppen were transferred from France in the spring of 1941 when the Wehrmacht attacked Yugoslavia and Greece, while seven more were transferred to the Soviet border for the Operation 'Barbarossa' in June 1941. Ju 87s enjoyed total superiority once more, helping to destroy over 1,500 Soviet aircraft, most of which were caught on the ground.

In 1942, anticipated replacement aircraft failed to materialize and Stuka production almost doubled that of the previous year. In 1943, an incredible 1,672 Stukas were produced but production fell away again in 1944 and finally ceased. Altogether, some 5,700 Ju 87s were produced.

Junkers Ju 88-4 of KG 76 (Heinz J. Nowarra).

JUNKERS JU 88

Type: *Light bomber;* **Crew:** *Two-six;* **Manufacturers:** *Junkers Flugzeug und Motorenwerke AG. Subcontracted by ATG, Opel, Volkswagen;* **Powerplant:** *(Ju 88-4/R) Two Junkers Jumo 211J-1;* **Dimensions:** *Span, 65 ft 10½ in (20.13 m); Length, 47 ft 2¼ in (14.4 m); Height, 15 ft 11 in (4.85 m);* **Weight:** *Empty, 17,637 lb (8,000 kg); Loaded, 26,700 lb (12,136 kg);* **Performance:** *Max speed, 273 mph (439 km/h) at 17,500 ft (5,335 m); Range, 1,553 miles (2,500 km); Ceiling, 27,880 ft (8,475 m);* **Armament:** *One forward-firing 20 mm MG FF cannon or two 7.9 mm MG 81 machine-guns and one 7.9 mm MG 81, one 7.9 mm MG 81 or 13 mm MG 131 and one MG 131 or two MG 81 firing aft. Bomb load (internal), 1,100 lb (500 kg) (external) four 550 lb (250 kg) bombs or two 2,200 lb (1,000 kg) bombs or torpedoes, plus two 550 lb bombs or 1,100 lb (500 kg) bombs.*

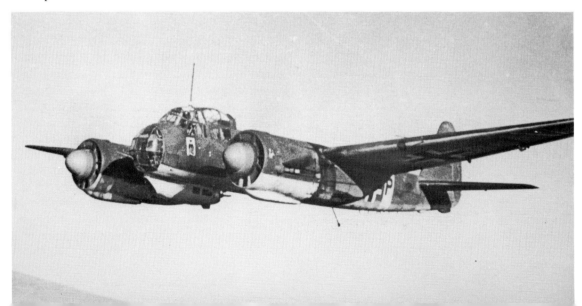

Junkers Ju 88-A-4 in northern Italy (Hans Heiri Stapfer).

This was by far the most successful of Germany's medium bombers during the Second World War, operating on all fronts with six different nations in a wide variety of roles including bombing, night fighting, night intrusion and torpedo bombing. The Ju 88 was even developed as a pilotless 'mistel' air-launched by FW 190s and Bf 109s during the Normandy invasion in June 1944.

Originally designed as a general-purpose aircraft and then for dive-bombing, the Ju 88 eventually emerged as a conventional twin engined monoplane bomber. Construction of

Below left *Junkers Ju 88D-1 of* Flugzeugführerschule (B) 16, *Magdeburg* (Heinz J. Nowarra).

Below *Junkers Ju 88S-1 powered by two BMW 801G-2 engines, which normally carried two 1,000 kg (2,205 lb) bombs on racks beneath the wing centre section* (Heinz J. Nowarra).

the first prototype was begun in 1936 and the Ju 88 V1 flew for the first time on 21 December of that year. Early in 1939 a pre-production consignment of 10 Ju 88A-0s were built for service trials. The first Ju 88 8A-1 made its maiden flight on 7 September 1939 and 60 production models were built by the end of the year. The Ju 88A-1 was capable of either level or dive-bombing.

The Ju 88 first entered service with the Luftwaffe in August/September 1939 and was among the first Luftwaffe types to drop bombs on British soil. Ju 88s also took part in the invasion of Norway and Denmark in April 1940, but played a minor supporting role to the Heinkel 111 during the successive campaign in the west in the spring of 1940. It was not until the opening phase in the Battle of Britain that

Junkers Ju 88-A-4 of the Edelweiss Geschwader *(Hans Heiri Stapfer).*

the Ju 88 was used in large numbers, some operating from as far afield as Denmark. They enjoyed early successes against RAF airfields and radar stations until 7 September when Reichsmarschal Göring redirected the German offensive against London. Despite high losses the Ju 88 Gruppen avoided the catastrophe attached to Heinkel III and Do 17 operations, largely because of its high speed.

The most important type was the Ju 88A-4, fitted with two 1,340 hp Junkers Jumo 2111J-I/J-2 radials, which began to replace the Ju 88A-1 on the production lines at the close of 1940. Span was increased by 6 ft (1.8 m) and the undercarriage was strengthened following failures on landing of earlier models. Experience gained during the Battle of Britain proved a need for additional armour plate and increased armament.

Lack of success with new designs led to the Ju 88 being adopted in a wide variety of roles. The Ju 88B with Jumo 213A radials did not enter production, but the Ju 88C-2 Zerstörer was adopted and fighter development continued with the C series. The Ju 88D-1 was a strategic reconnaissance version of the A-4 with three cameras in the bomb bay. The Ju 88P, which appeared in 1942-43, was intended as an anti-tank aircraft, fitted with a 75 mm BK 7.5 anti-tank gun in the nose, but it was first used, unsuccessfully, as a day interceptor over the Reich. It also failed in its intended role before

being relegated to operations in support of the Wehrmacht on the Eastern Front.

By mid-1943 the A series had become increasingly vulnerable when used on daylight operations and the S series was developed to improve performance. The Ju 88S-1 was fitted with 1,700 hp BMW 801G engines with GM-1 power boost and a completely re-designed glazed nose. An offshoot of the basic Ju 88 design was the Ju 188 with extended, pointed wingtips and a completely redesigned forward fuselage. Production continued until the end of the war, by which time almost 15,000 Ju 88s, including over 10,700 bomber and reconnaissance types, had been produced.

MARTIN B-10, B-12

Type: *Light bomber;* **Crew:** *Four;* **Manufacturers:** *Glenn L. Martin Co, Cleveland, Ohio;* **Powerplant:** *(YB-12) Two Pratt & Whitney R-1690-11 Hornets;* **Dimensions:** *Span, 70 ft 6 in (21.48 m); Length, 45 ft 3 in (13.81 m); Height, (B-10B) 15 ft 5 in (4.72 m);* **Weight:** *(B-10B) Empty, 9,681 lb (4,400 kg); Loaded, 16,400 lb (7,454 kg);* **Performance:** *(B-10B) Max speed, 213 mph (340 km/h); Ceiling, 24,200 ft (7,378 m); Range, 1,240 miles (1,996 km);* **Armament:** *Three 0.3 in Browning machine-guns. Bomb load, 1,000 lb (454 kg).*

The Martin B-10, which in the 1930s introduced revolutionary features such as retractable undercarriage, gun turret and cantilever monoplane design.

The Glenn L. Martin Co, which had had a very successful partnership with the US Army in the 1920s, was determined to be among the main suppliers of the next generation of all-metal, twin-engined, monoplane bombers. With this in mind, they developed the Model 123 as a private venture. Although the Boeing B-9 emerged slightly ahead of the Martin Model, the latter had the added advantage of an internal bomb bay and was the first US bomber to have a front gun turret fitted.

The prototype Model 123 was delivered to the US Army on 20 March 1932 and designated XB-907 for trials at Wright Field. In later trials at Wright Field in October 1932, the improved Martin XB-907A, despite the recent addition of the front gun turret, achieved a speed of 207 mph (333 km/h) at 6,000 ft (1,829 m), far faster than the fastest US fighter of the day. An official order for 48 aircraft was issued on 17 January 1933.

Deliveries of the first production Martin 139 models started in June 1934. This version introduced two enclosed cockpits for the pilot and radio-operator/rear gunner. The first 14 aircraft were designated YB-10 and they were followed by seven YB-12s with more powerful Hornet radial engines. A bomb bay tank for long range flights was installed in the 25 B-12As. Two experimental models included in the original 1933 order raised the top speed to 236 mph (380 km/h) at 25,000 ft (7,621 m).

In 1931 the US Army Air Corps was charged with Coastal defence and several YB-10s and B-12s were fitted with floats for operation on water. A total of 109 B-10s (the last in 1942!) followed, before the type was replaced by the B-17 and B-18. Also 189 versions were exported. Martin 139s were flown by Chinese pilots in raids on the Japanese mainland in 1938 and 120 supplied to the Dutch were used in the Netherlands East Indies during opening engagements with Japanese fighters in the Second World War.

MARTIN B-26 MARAUDER

Type: *Medium bomber;* **Crew:** *Seven;* **Manufacturers:** *Glenn L. Martin Co, Baltimore, Maryland (except B-26C) and Omaha, Nebraska (B-26C only);* **Powerplant:** *(B-26C) Two Pratt & Whitney R-2800-43;* **Dimensions:** *Span, 71 ft (21.64 m); Length, 58 ft 3 in (17.75 m); Height, 21 ft 6 in (6.55 m);* **Weight:** *Empty, 24,000 lb (10,909 kg); Loaded, 38,200 lb (17,340 kg);* **Performance:** *Max speed, 282 mph (454 km/h) at 15,000 ft (4,573 m); Ceiling, 21,700 ft (6,615 m); Range, 1,150 miles (1,850 km);* **Armament:** *12 .5 in machine-guns. Bomb load, 3,000 lb (1,363 kg).*

The Martin Marauder was designed to a specification issued by the Air Corps on 25 January 1939 for a new high-speed medium bomber. On 5 July 1939, the Martin 179 design beat competitive designs and the USAAC ordered 201 of the type in September without the benefit of prototypes or testing. The first B-26 came off the production lines on 25 November 1939 and the first test flights seemed to herald great promise. However, its high landing speed and an increase in gross weight on the B-26A resulted in many accidents during early test and training flights. The Marauder gained an unwelcome reputation for being an unsafe aircraft. It became known as a 'widow-maker' and 'flying whore' because it had no visible means of support (a reference to its small wing area).

On 8 December 1941, the day following the Japanese attack on the United States Pacific Fleet at Pearl Harbor, 53 of the first 56 Marauders took off from Langley Field, Virginia for Australia. These B-26A Marauders formed the 22nd Bomb Group and in April 1942 they saw action for the first time, during attacks on New Guinea. During 1942, B-26As saw wide-ranging service, being employed as torpedo bombers in the Battle of Midway in June and, based in Alaska, for long-range strikes on the Aleutians. Although these raids were good for morale, the bomb loads were of necessity small, because of the need to carry extra fuel in bomb bay tanks.

The B-26B, which began production in May 1942, introduced armour plate around the pilot's area and improved armament. A ventral tunnel gun and a new tail gun position were added. On the B-26B-10, improvements were made to the flying characteristics by adding a taller fin and rudder and increasing the wing area and wing span. The B-26B grew even heavier with the installation of a second nose

Right *Martin B-26B-40 Marauder 42-43304 Marlin of the 444th Bomb Squadron, 320th Bomb Group, 9th Air Force (USAF).*

Below *Martin B-26C-45 Marauder of the 450th Bomb Squadron, 322nd Bomb Group, 9th Air Force (USAF).*

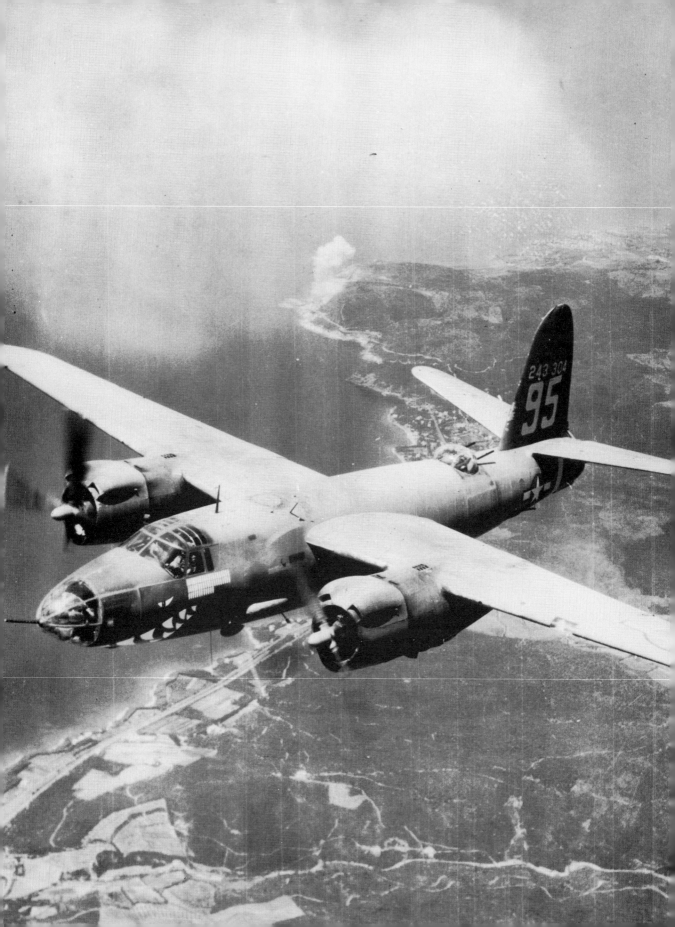

gun, two blister guns each side of the fuselage below the cockpit and a Martin-Bell power-operated turret. Some 1,242 B-26Bs were built at Baltimore and a further 1,235 B-26Cs, which were not dissimilar, were built at a second factory at Omaha, Nebraska.

Marauders began equipping the US 8th Air Force in England in the spring of 1943. But their second mission, on 14 May 1943, ended in disaster when 10 out of 11 B-26s failed to return from a low-level strike on Ijmuiden, Holland. During the summer of 1943, Marauders were switched to a high-level bombing role but success was only finally achieved late in 1943, when all B-26 groups were transferred to the 9th Air Force for tactical support of the Allied build-up to the invasion of Europe.

Marauders also fought in the Mediterranean Theatre with the USAAF and the RAF. Under the terms of Lend-Lease, about 522 Marauders were handed over to the RAF and SAAF. In RAF service the Marauder served exclusively in the Mediterranean Theatre from August 1942, equipping two RAF and five SAAF squadrons of the Desert Air Force and taking part in the Allied invasions of Sicily, Italy and Sardinia.

The B-26F had the wing incidence angle increased slightly in an effort to improve take-off performance further. Some 300 were built before minor internal changes altered the designation to B-26G. Some 893 Gs were built before deliveries ceased in March 1945. Altogether, some 5,266 Marauders were built, of which 1,585 were built in Omaha, Nebraska and 3,681 in Baltimore.

Martin B-26 Marauders of the Free French Air Force on Sardinia (Hans Heiri Stapfer).

MCDONNELL DOUGLAS A-3D SKYWARRIOR/B-66 DESTROYER

Type: *(A3D) carrier-borne strategic bomber; (B-66) Tactical strike bomber;* **Crew:** *Three;* **Manufacturers:** *Douglas Aircraft Co, Long Beach and Tulsa;* **Powerplant:** *(A-3) Two Pratt & Whitney J57-10 turbojets; (B-66B) Two Allison J71-A-13 turbojets;* **Dimensions:** *Span, 72 ft 6 in (22.1 m); Length, 75 ft 2 in (22.9 m); Height, 23 ft 7 in (7.16 m);* **Weight:** *Empty, (A-3) 39,409 lb (17,875 kg) (B-66B) 42,369 lb (19,218 kg); Loaded, (A-3) 82,000 lb (37,195 kg) (B-66B) 83,000 lb (37,648 kg);* **Performance:** *Max speed (B-66B) 594 mph (956 km/h) at 36,000 ft (10,975 m); Range 1,500 miles (2,415 km); Ceiling, 43,000 ft (13,109 m);* **Armament:** *(B-66B) Two 20 mm cannon in radar-controlled GE tail turret. Bomb load, (B-66) 15,000 lb (6,818 kg). (A-3) 12,000 lb (5,454 kg).*

In 1948, the US Navy invited tenders from US aircraft manufacturers for a carrier-borne jet bomber capable of carrying nuclear weapons. One of the restrictions imposed was a weight limitation of 100,000 lb (45,454 kg) to enable it to fly from projected super-carriers then being considered. Ed Heinemann's design weighed in at only 68,000 lb (30,909 kg), thus allowing it to be flown from smaller US carriers then in service. On 31 March 1949, Douglas were awarded a contract for two prototype XA-3D-1 Skywarriors. The XA-3D-1 flew on 28 October 1952, but the J40 engines were subsequently replaced by the more powerful Pratt & Whitney J57. Although the supercarrier was cancelled in 1949 it was adopted in the early 1950s, and the weight of the A-3 could then be increased to 84,000 lb (38,181 kg).

The first five production A-3D-1 Skywarriors entered service with VAH-1 (Heavy Attack Squadron) of the US Navy at NAS Jacksonville on 31 March 1956. The first of 164 A3D-2 bombers, with two improved J57-P-10 turbojets and accommodation for two Mk.28 hydrogen bombs, entered service early in 1957. The bombers were strengthened for LABS (Low Altitude Bombing System). Altogether, some 283 Skywarriors were built before production ceased in January 1961. In their time they have performed several roles, including bomber, reconnaissance, tanker, trainer and passenger transport.

When the USAF began showing interest in a tactical light bomber and reconnaissance aircraft, Douglas thought it had a ready-made answer in a land-based version of the A-3. Outwardly, the Douglas Model 1326 looked exactly the same aircraft. The new model retained a three man crew and the General Electric electronic fire-control system which operated two 20 mm tail guns. The powerplant selected was the Pratt & Whitney J57. However, as development became more protracted and expensive the B-66 emerged as a completely new aircraft.

B-66 production centred on the Long Beach facility of the Douglas Aircraft Company's Aircraft Division. No prototypes were built but

Background photograph *A3D-2 Skywarrior of the US Navy (Douglas).*

Inset below left *Douglas RB-66 4450 of the USAF (Douglas).*

Inset below *Douglas EKA-3B electronic jammer and tanker version of the Skywarrior (McDonnell Douglas).*

Douglas RB-66 Destroyers in formation (USAF).

five RB-66As, designed for all-weather night-photographic reconnaissance, were built for evaluation. The first RB-66B flew from Long Beach to Edwards AFB on 28 June 1954. The Air Force accepted the first operational RB-66B on 1 February 1956.

The B-66B, specially designed to permit a wide selection of bomb combinations for a variety of missions, including nuclear strike, made its initial flight on 4 January 1955. Deliveries of 72 B-66Bs to the USAF began on 16 March 1956. A B-66B took part in Operation 'Redwing', the H-Bomb drop at the Bikini atoll.

The RB-66C was an electronic reconnaissance aircraft similar to the RB-66B. It made its maiden flight on 29 October 1955 and entered service on 11 May 1956. Some 36 RB-66Cs were produced at the Douglas, Tulsa, plant before production was switched to the WB-66D electronic weather reconnaissance version. The first of 36 WB-66Ds was delivered on 26 June 1957, the last in September 1958.

Production of the Destroyer finished in June 1958 but many were rebuilt as EB-66E tactical

ECM and ESM aircraft. The EB-66E served for a short time during the early 1970s in the war in South-east Asia. Also some 85 A-3Bs had a 3,355 gallon fuel tank installed in their bomb bays and were redesignated KA-3B 'Whale'. They saved hundreds of American aircraft in Vietnam operating as aerial tankers. A further 36 A-3Bs had ECM equipment installed in the forward part of their bomb bays and were redesignated EKA-3B. These operated in South-east Asia until the end of the Vietnam War in 1973.

At least 40 Skywarriors are still serving with the US Navy as aerial tankers and FEW (Fleet Electronic Warfare) aircraft and with Reserve units. It is anticipated that many will still be serving operational squadrons and as flying test beds until the 1990s, some 40 years since its design!

NORTH AMERICAN (ROCKWELL) A-5A (A3J-1) VIGILANTE

Type: *Supersonic carrier-borne strike aircraft;* **Crew:** *Two;* **Manufacturers:** *North American Aviation (Rockwell International), Columbus, Ohio;* **Powerplant:** *Two 16,150 lb (7,340 kg) st General Electric J79-2/-4 turbojets;* **Dimensions:** *Span, 53 ft (16.15 m); Length, 75 ft 10 in (23.11 m); Height, 19 ft 5 in (5.92 m);* **Weight:** *Empty, 38,000 lb (17,240 kg); Loaded, 80,000 lb (36,285 kg);* **Performance:** *Max speed, 1,385 mph (2,230 km/h) (Mach 2.1); Service ceiling, 67,000 ft (20,400 m).*

The Vigilante was the last aircraft designed as a Mach 2 long-range strategic strike aircraft for carrier operation. In 1954 the US Navy had taken up the offer of a North American proposal for a NAGPAW (North American General-Purpose Attack Weapon), which called for an all-weather bomber capable of nuclear delivery using the LABS (low-altitude bombing system).

The first of two A3J-1 prototypes flew on 31 August 1958 and a production contract ensued

North American Vigilante on the deck of the since-decommissioned USS Intrepid moored at New York and open to the public.

in January 1959. The A3J-1 was designed to carry either a Mk 27 nuclear weapon externally or a Mk 28 stored in an internal 'linear' bomb bay, from which the weapon could be ejected via a tunnel between the engine jet-pipes. However, problems with the internal bay were never solved and it was subsequently used as a storage area for additional fuel tanks. The A-5B, of which six were built, carried additional fuel behind the bombardier-navigator's cockpit and in extra drop tanks below the wings.

Deliveries of the A3J-1 (A-5A) to the US Navy began in June 1961, and the first full squadron deployment at sea was with VAH-7 aboard the USS *Enterprise* in August 1962. However, with the cancellation of the US Navy's strategic nuclear strike role in 1962 in favour of the Polaris missile 59, early production A-5As and A-5Bs were converted to RA-5C multi-sensor reconnaissance aircraft. Many gave valuable service in the war in South-east Asia. The last of 156 Vigilantes was delivered in November 1970. The 'Vigi' remains the only supersonic carrier-borne aircraft to serve with the US Navy.

NORTH AMERICAN B-25 MITCHELL

Type: *Medium bomber;* **Crew:** *Three-six;* **Manufacturers:** *(B-25A-C/E-H) North American Aviation, Inglewood, California. (B-25D,J) Kansas City;* **Powerplant:** *(B-25J) Two Wright R-2600-29 Double Cyclones;* **Dimensions:** *Span, 67 ft 7 in (20.6 m); Length, 52 ft 11 in (16.1 m); Height, 16 ft 4 in (5 m);* **Weight:** *Empty, 19,480 lb (8,854 kg); Loaded, 35,000 lb (15,909 kg);* **Performance:** *Max speed, 272 mph (438 km/h) at 13,000 ft (3,963 m); Ceiling, 24,200 ft (7,378 m); Range, 1,350 miles (2,173 km);* **Armament:** *(B-25H) 14 .5 in machine-guns and one 75 mm cannon. Bomb load, 2,000 lb (909 kg) torpedo or 3,200 lb (1,454 kg) bombs.*

The B-25 Mitchell was the result of an Air Corps requirement for a medium bomber in 1938. North American built the NA-40-1 prototype as a private venture and successive improvements led to the NA-62. In September 1939, the Air Corps placed an order for 184 B-25s. The first flying example took to the air on 19 August 1940.

The B-25A, of which 40 were built, introduced self-sealing tanks and armour plate. In 1941 the first B-25As began equipping the 17th Bomb Group (medium). During an anti-shipping strike off the west coast of America on 24 December a B-25A of this group sank a Japanese submarine.

Some 120 B-25B models were built. Externally, it differed from previous models in having Bendix electric turrets and the tail gun deleted. A total of 23 B-25Bs were delivered to the RAF and a few more went to Russia. In April 1942 B-25Bs of the 3rd Bomb Group in the Philippines were used against Japanese targets. That same month, 16 B-25Bs led by Lt Col (later General) James H. Doolittle were flown off the deck of the carrier *USS Hornet* for raids on the Japanese mainland 800 miles distant. Most aircraft crash-landed in China and Doolittle was awarded the Medal of Honor.

Mitchell production increased with a second North American factory at Dallas, Texas, turning out B-25Ds. Dallas ultimately built 2,290 Ds while Inglewood turned out 1,619 of the not dissimilar B-25C. The majority of the 800 Mitchells delivered to the RAF were Mk IIs which were the equivalent of the B-25C. The RAF employed the Mitchell primarily as a light day-bomber.

North American also built 405 B-25Gs and 1,000 B-25Hs which were both fitted with a nose-firing 75 mm cannon for anti-shipping strikes in the Pacific. The B-25H first entered service in the Pacific in February 1944. Cannons were not successful, however, and the type was withdrawn in August 1944. The B-25J, of which 4,318 models were built at Kansas City by 1945, introduced four .5 in 'blister' guns, two on each side of the fuselage below the cockpit. The majority of USAAF B-25Js fought in the south-west Pacific where they replaced the B-26 in squadron service. In RAF service the B-25J was known as the Mitchell III, and equipped six squadrons in No 2

Left *North American B-25J Mitchell 44-28844 (USAF).*

Inset *North American B-25D Mitchell (USAF).*

North American B-25H Mitchell 43-4570 (USAF).

Group and 2nd TAF and two PR units.

During 1943-44, 60 B-25s were stripped and modified to serve as AT-24A-D and TB-25D-J advanced trainers. TB-25Js were finally retired from service in January 1959 and the last transport version was retired in May 1960. Almost 11,000 examples of the Mitchell were built, including some 9,816 which served in the USAAF.

ROCKWELL INTERNATIONAL B-1

Type: *Strategic bomber and missile launcher;* **Crew:** *Four;* **Manufacturers:** *Rockwell International Corp, Palmdale, California;* **Powerplant:** *Four General Electric F101-GE-102 turbofans;* **Dimensions:** *Span, (swept) 78 ft 2 in (23.84 m), (spread) 136 ft 8 in (41.67 m); Length, 147 ft (44.81 m);* **Weight:** *Loaded, 477,000 lb (216,365 kg);* **Performance:** *Max speed, Mach 1.25; Penetration speed, 600 mph+ (965 km/h);* **Armament:** *Provision for 22 AGM-86B ALCM missiles (8 internally and 14 externally) or 38 SRAMs or, conventional/nuclear bomb load, 75,000 lb (internal) and 40,000 lb (external).*

In November 1969, after 20 years of study, the USAF finally issued a requirement to replace the B-52. The new aircraft had to be able to take off from dispersed, small air bases and yet be able to cruise to its target at subsonic speed and at low altitude before changing to high altitude, high speed over the target area.

North American Rockwell won the B-1 variable-geometry aircraft contract for three prototypes on 5 June 1970. The first B-1A was rolled out on 26 October 1974 and flew for the first time on 23 December. Mach 2 was exceeded for the first time in April 1976. As expenditure rocketed, American chiefs of staff looked to cruise missiles such as the AGM-109 Tomahawk, eight of which could be carried inside a modified B-52 and launched from outside enemy airspace. On 30 June 1977, the B-1 programme was cancelled by President Carter (although testing continued with three more B-1As having flown by 1978).

The B-1 project was subsequently reinstated by the Reagan administration in 1981, although the original SAC requirement for 241 aircraft was reduced to 100 of the B-1B model. This differs from the B-1A in having a higher maximum take-off weight, reduced radar signature and the use of radar absorbing material in certain parts of the airframe. A unique struc-

Rockwell B-1B intercontinental bomber (Rockwell International).

tural mode control system (SMCS), using small canard foreplanes and the bottom rudder section, minimizes the effect of turbulence on crew and airframe during high-speed, low level, terrain-following. Variable geometry inlets, which would have allowed speeds of up to Mach 2.1, were eliminated as a cost-cutting manoeuvre.

The B-1B prototype (second converted B-1 prototype) flew for the first time on 23 March 1983. The first production B-1B flew on 18 October 1984 and the ninth B-1B introduced a movable bulkhead in the forward weapons bay, enabling it to carry eight AGM-86 air-launched cruise missiles (ALCM), SRAMS and additional internal fuel tanks. Deliveries of the first 29 aircraft began on 29 June 1985 to the 96th Bomb Wing at Dyess AFB, Texas, and the wing became operational in September 1986. Ellsworth, South Carolina, received 35 B-1Bs and Grand Forks, North Dakota, 17 aircraft. The last unit to be equipped with the B-1B was the 384th Bomb Wing at McConnell in Kansas, which received 17 aircraft. The 100th B-1B was delivered to the USAF on 30 April 1988.

Initially, the B-1Bs are being used in the penetration role, until relieved by the Northrop B-2 Advanced Technology Bomber from about 1992. The B-1Bs will then be used as stand-off cruise missile launchers, taking over from B-52Hs, which in turn will displace the B-52G in the conventional bomber/minelayer role.

SHORT STIRLING I-III

Type: *Heavy bomber*; **Crew:** *Seven-eight*; **Manufacturers:** *Short Brothers Ltd, Rochester, Kent. Subcontracted by Short and Harland, Belfast and Austin, Longbridge;* **Powerplant:** *(I) Four Bristol Hercules XI. (II) Wright R-2600-A5B Cyclone. (III) Bristol Hercules XVI;* **Dimensions:** *Span, 99 ft 1 in (30.2 m); Length, 87 ft 3 in (26.6 m); Height, 22 ft 9 in (6.94 m);* **Weight:** *(III) Empty, 46,900 lb (21,273 kg); Loaded, 70,000 lb (31,750 kg);* **Performance:** *Max speed, 270 mph (435 km/h); Service ceiling, 17,000 ft (5,182 m); Range (III), 590 miles (950 km) with 14,000 lb bombs, 2,010 miles (3,235 km) with 3,500 lb;* **Armament:** *Two .303 in Brownings in nose and dorsal turrets and four in tail turret. Bomb load, 18,000 lb (8,165 kg).*

Although chiefly remembered for its short span, high-legged undercarriage and long fuselage, the Stirling was the first four-engined monoplane bomber to be used operationally during the Second World War and as such shouldered much of the early RAF bombing offensive burden, taking part in the early daylight offensive and all three 1,000 bomber raids in 1942. Its extremely rugged construction, four-engine safety and high manoeuvrability (it could out-turn fighters and could even be looped) made it extremely popular with crews.

Unlike its brothers in arms, the Halifax, Manchester and Lancaster, which were originally intended for twin-engine layout, the Stirling was designed from the outset as a four-engined bomber. Air Ministry Specification B.12/36 in July 1936 called for a long-range strategic bomber capable of carrying a 4,000 lb (1,814 kg) bomb load a distance of 2,000 miles (3,218 km). It also stipulated that the new bomber should have a wing span no greater than 100 ft (30.48 m) in order that it could be accommodated in the standard RAF hangars

of the day. Unfortunately, the heavy-structure and low aspect ratio wing which resulted severely restricted the aircraft's operational ceiling.

The Air Ministry accepted Arthur Gouge's design and ordered two prototypes from Shorts and two from Supermarine. The latter's aircraft were never finished, the partially completed models being destroyed in a German air raid in 1940. Meanwhile, in April 1938 Shorts received an initial production contract for 100

S.29 Stirlings. The Company built a half-scale model, named the Short S.31, which first flew on 19 September 1938, powered by four Pobjoy Niagara engines, and this provided valuable aeronautical data. Tests revealed the need to increase wing incidence but tooling for full-scale production had already started, so Shorts extended the undercarriage.

The wing on the Stirling prototype owed much to the company's long experience in flying-boat design and incorporated Gouge-designed flaps which, when extended, provided increased wing area. Unfortunately, two deep girders used to support the fuselage deck indicated that the bomb bay had to be divided into three narrow sections which meant that the type could never carry bombs bigger than 4,000 lb (1,814 kg). Additional bombs could be carried in three cells in each wing centre section.

The first prototype took off from Rochester on 14 May 1939 powered by Hercules II air-cooled engines. The flight was without incident, but the undercarriage collapsed on landing and the aircraft was written off. The second prototype began flight trials with a modified and strengthened undercarriage and flew for the first time on 3 December 1939. The first production Stirling from the Rochester factory flew on 7 May, while the first Belfast-built Stirling flew on 18 October. The first 10 Rochester-built production models were classed as Stirling trainers as a result of their low-powered 1,375 hp Hercules II engines. Hercules IIIs, Xs but mostly XIs, were fitted to subsequent Mk I Stirlings, the first of which was delivered to No 7 Squadron at Leeming, Yorkshire on 29 August 1940.

Problems plagued the entry of the Stirling into squadron service, and it was not until the night of 10/11 February 1941 that No 7 Squadron mounted its first operation, when three Stirling Is took off from Oakington, Cambridgeshire, for a raid on Rotterdam. On 17/18 April a lone Stirling from No 7

Stirling III BF 509 (Shorts).

Squadron bombed Berlin, and the first daylight sortie, against Emden, took place on 27 April. That month No 15 Squadron at Wyton converted to the Stirling. Altogether, the Stirling was to serve with a dozen squadrons of RAF Bomber Command.

Early operational experience with the Stirling I led to changes in defensive armament. Originally, Frazer-Nash nose and retractable ventral turrets housed twin Brownings while the tail turret carried four Brownings. The ventral turret soon gave way to pivoted pairs of Brownings in special beam hatches which in turn were replaced with a FN dorsal turret.

Throughout 1941, Stirlings made daylight attacks on German capital ships and attacked targets as far afield as northern Italy and Pilsen in Czechoslovakia. In July, Stirlings of No 3 Group took over from Blenheims of No 2 Group in a series of fighter-escorted 'Circus' operations over France. These daylight incursions were designed to lure the *Luftwaffe* to battle but were short-lived, and the Stirlings soon reverted to night operations. Raids on Italy in September meant crossing the Alps and this proved a dangerous obstacle for Stirling crews, only too aware of their machine's inability to climb much above 12,000 ft (3,678 m) with a full load of fuel and bombs.

Although assembly lines had opened at Austin Motors in June 1941, by the end of the year Stirling production, never high throughout the war, suffered a blow when a contract for 140 Canadian-built Stirling B Mk IIs powered by Wright Cyclone R-2600-A5B engines was cancelled after only two prototypes and three production models had been built. The Stirling did, however, become standard equipment throughout No 3 Group, which gradually replaced its ageing Wellingtons with the type. During the winter of 1941-42 Stirlings were fitted with 'Trinity', an early blind bombing radar aid, later fully developed as 'Oboe', and in August Stirlings of No 7 Squadron joined the newly formed Pathfinder force and participated in the first PFF operation over Flensburg.

The Stirling III entered production in 1942, fitted with the 1,635 hp Hercules XVI powerplant with underslung oil coolers, but the increase in performance over the B Mk I was marginal. The B Mk III differed from the Mk I in having a Lancaster type FN50 dorsal turret, larger fuel tanks and an improved interior design. In an effort to improve performance, Group Captain (later Air Vice Marshal) Don Bennett, chief of 8 Group (PFF), ordered that all No 7 Squadron's Stirlings be stripped of all excess weight, including armour-plate.

Two posthumous VCs were awarded to members of Stirling crews. The first recipient was Flight Sergeant R.H. Middleton (RAAF) of No 149 Squadron who, despite being mortally wounded, remained at the controls after a raid on the Fiat Works at Turin on the night of 28/29 November 1942, thus allowing his crew to parachute to safety, before he crashed into the sea. The second recipient was Flight Sergeant A.L. Aaron, pilot of 218 Squadron Stirling. He saved his crew on the night of 12/13 August 1943 when he nursed his bomber back on three engines, only to die as a result of his terrible injuries sustained on the raid on Turin.

Many crews were thankful for the Stirling's rugged construction which allowed them to return to base with shattered fuselages and shredded wings. In the summer of 1943, when it fell from grace as a heavy bomber, the Stirling was frequently used on less heavily defended targets, such as VI sites in northern France and also for 'gardening' (mine-laying) operations. The final bombing operation was carried out on 8 September 1944, when 149 Squadron bombed Le Havre. The Stirling IV gave excellent service as a glider tug and flying tanker, and the Mk V served equally well as a long-range transport. Others were used throughout the war on spy-dropping and radio and radar-

Above right *Short Stirling Mk I of No 7 Squadron, RAF Oakington, Cambridgeshire (Chas E. Brown).*

Right *Stirling Mk V PK 178 modified for Far East Transport Duties (Long).*

jamming operations. Altogether, 2,221 Stirlings I-IV were built, flying a total of 18,440 operational sorties.

SAVOIA-MARCHETTI SM-79

Type: *Bomber, torpedo-bomber and reconnaissance aircraft;* **Crew:** *Four-five;* **Manufacturers:** *SIAI 'Savoia-Marchetti'. Built under licence by Aeronautica Macchi and OM 'Reggiane'. (79 JR) Industria Aeronautica Romana, Romania;* **Powerplant:** *(SM-79-II) Three Piaggio P.XI RC 40;* **Dimensions:** *Span, 69 ft 6½ in (21.2 m); Length, 53 ft 1¾ in (16.2 m); Height, 13 ft 5½ in (4.1 m);* **Weight:** *Empty, 16,755 lb (7,600 kg); Loaded, 24,912 lb (11,323 kg);* **Performance:** *Max speed, 270 mph (434 km/h) at 12,000 ft (3,658 m); Range, 1,243 miles (2,000 km); Ceiling, 22,966 ft (7,001 m);* **Armament:** *Three 12.7 mm Breda SAFAT machine-guns and one 7.7 mm Lewis machine-gun. Internal bomb load up to 2,200 lb (1,000 kg) or two 450 mm torpedoes externally.*

The Savoia-Marchetti SM-79 Sparviero (Hawk) was the most successful land-based torpedo bomber of the war and was produced in greater numbers than all other Italian multi-engined bombers combined. A development of the SM-81 Pipistrello, the civil prototype SM-79, flew for the first time late in 1934. Despite mixed construction methods—the fuselage comprised steel tube alloy with wood and fabric covering while the wings were of wood and fabic covered—the new aircraft proved robust and reliable and by 1936 had established many new speed records.

Late in 1936, the SM-79-I bomber version, powered by three Alfa Romeo 126 RC 34 radial engines, entered service with the Regia Aeronautica. Externally it differed little from the civil version but was fitted with a streamlined machine-gun fairing above the cockpit and a ventral gondola was added to accommodate the bombardier. The twin-engined SM-79B was developed in 1936 and small numbers were exported to Brazil, Iraq and Romania, where the 79-JR was built under licence with two Junkers Jumo 211Da engines. The Romanians used the SM-79-JR extensively on the Russian Front. An order was also placed by Yugoslavia for the SM-79-I version.

The SM-79-I saw service with two Fast Bomber Groups in the Spanish Civil War where it proved highly successful. Early in 1937 it was considered for the Italian torpedo-bombing squadrons, the 'Aerosiluranti'. In August 1938,

Savoia-Marchetti SM-79 of the Royal Hungarian Air Force (Ödön Horvath via Hans Heiri Stapfer).

Westland-built Sopwith 1½ Strutter (Westland).

trials were carried out with the SM-79 carrying two air-launched torpedoes. These proved successful and the SM-79-II entered production in October 1939 with the more powerful 1,000 hp Piaggio P.XI RC 40 engines to improve performance.

By the time of Italy's intervention in the Second World War, on 10 June 1940, just over 400 SM-79s were in first-line service with the Regia Aeronautica. They enjoyed most success in the torpedo-bombing role in the Mediterranean, but many were also used for strategic reconnaissance, gravity bombing and close-support missions in North Africa. A few SM-79-III versions fitted with a forward-firing 20 mm cannon were built bringing total Sparviero production in Italy to some 1,300 (including export models).

SOPWITH 1½ STRUTTER

Type: *Day bomber;* **Crew:** *One-Two;* **Manufacturers:** *Sopwith Aviation, Kingston-on-Thames. Subcontracted by Mann Egerton, Norwich and Westland Aircraft, Yeovil;* **Powerplant:** *One Clerget rotary engine;* **Dimensions:** *Span, 33 ft 6 in (10.2 m); Length, 25 ft 3 in (7.6 m); Height, 10 ft 3 in (3.1 m);* **Weight:** *(Two-seater) Loaded, 2,350 lb (1,065 kg);* **Performance:** *(Two-seater) Max speed, 92 mph (148 km/h) at 12,000 ft (3,658 m);* **Armament:** *(Single-seat bomber) One Vickers machine-gun firing forward. Bomb load, 260 lb (118 kg).*

In 1915, the Sopwith Aviation Company

prepared drawings for a two-seat biplane which was destined to become one of the most significant aircraft of the First World War. The aircraft, first designated Type 9700, was not designed to have fixed front-gun armament, but fortunately it proved unusually well-suited to the employment of such armament once interrupter gears became available.

The prototype aircraft was built during the last few weeks of 1915 and the Royal Naval Air Service received its first Type 9700 early in 1916. The RNAS pioneered the type as a single-seat bomber carrying a bomb load of 224 lb and also used it as a fighter escort. Initially, the Admiralty ordered 150 Type 9700s and the RFC subsequently ordered the Sopwith Two-Seater, as it was known in this service. Universally, it is known as the Sopwith 1½ Strutter, a designation believed to have been arrived at as a result of the type's unusual arrangement of long and short pairs of centre-section struts. Two other notable features were a tailplane of variable incidence and hinged flap airbrakes in the lower wing roots.

The 1½ Strutter first entered service on the Western Front early in 1916 and was immediately successful as a fighter, a bomber and two-seat reconnaissance aircraft. It was also the first operational British aircraft with a synchronized machine-gun. With the arrival of newer German fighters in the late summer of 1916, the 1½ Strutter was relegated to bombing and reconnaissance operations. The type was obsolescent by the spring of 1917, but it continued to give valuable service with the RNAS on other fronts and it was also used on anti U-boat patrols. The RNAS pioneered the type as a single-seat bomber carrying 260 lb (118 kg) bomb loads. As a two-seater with the RFC it could only carry a bomb load of some 130 lb (60 kg) because it was very difficult to carry and successfully aim bombs on and from the two-seat 1½ Strutter. In March 1918, a 1½ Strutter became the first two-seat aircraft to take off from a British warship. By the end of the war, 170 1½ Strutters were still in service with the RAF and France had built 4,200 under licence.

TUPOLEV TU-16 BADGER

Type: *Strategic bomber;* **Crew:** *5-6* **Manufacturer:** *Design Bureau of André N. Tupolev;* **Powerplant:** *Two Mikulin AM-3M turbojets;* **Dimensions:** *Span, 109 ft (33.5 m); Length, 114 ft 2 in (34.8 m); Height, 35 ft 6 in (10.8 m);* **Weight:** *Empty, about 72,750 lb (33,000 kg); Loaded, about 150,000 lb (68,000 kg);* **Performance:** *Max speed 587 mph (945 km/h); Ceiling, 39,370 ft (12,003 m); Range, 3,580 miles (5,764 km);* **Armament:** *Six/seven 23 mm NR-23 cannon. Internal bomb load of 19,800 lb (9,000 kg).*

The prototype Tu-88 was designed to meet a Soviet need for a long-range strategic bomber in the same mould as the British V-Bomber force. Very much a contemporary of the Valiant, the Tu-88, which flew for the first time in 1952, was more heavily armed. Technologically, it lagged behind, depending on the early Tu-4 (B-29 copy) for much of its electronic and system development.

Above *A Tu-16 Badger is closely shadowed by an F-4 Phantom of CVW-11 during fleet operations in 1975 (US Navy).*

Below *Tupolev Tu-16 Badger viewed from the cockpit of a Royal Norwegian Air Force fighter over the Baltic (RNAF).*

Deliveries of the Tu-16 to the Soviet Air Force took place over about five years, between 1954-59. The Badger-A could carry a bomb load of 19,841 lb (9,000 kg). The Badger-B served with the AV-MF (Soviet Navy) and was fitted with underwing pylons for carrying two Kennel anti-shipping missiles. The Badger-C, which was first seen at the 1961 Soviet Aviation Day, was equipped with search radar in a chin radome and carried a Kipper stand-off bomb which partly protruded from the weapons bay under the fuselage. The Tu-16D was a maritime reconnaissance version and the Badger-E, an electronic reconnaissance type. Later versions were updates of earlier models converted for ECM and ESM missions. Many Tu-16s were also converted to tankers for the air-refuelling role.

Production of the Tu-16 finished around 1959, by which time about 2,000 models had been built. The type was also exported to Egypt (which used them as airborne missile launchers in the war with Israel in 1973), Indonesia, Iraq and China, where it continued in production for many years.

Around 307 ageing Badgers were still serving with the LRA (Long Range Aviation) in the bomber/tanker/ECM/Elint role late in 1986. At the same time, 115 Badgers were serving with Frontal Aviation (similar to the USAF Tactical Air Command). Naval Aviation had almost 400 Badgers on strength, including 240 in the strike role, 80 in the maritime reconnaissance/ASW role and about 75 in the tanker role.

TUPOLEV TU-20 (TU-95) BEAR

Type: *Strategic bomber;* **Crew:** *5-6* **Manufacturers:** *Design Bureau of André N. Tupolev;* **Powerplant:** *Four Kuznetsov Nk-12M turboprops;* **Dimensions:** *Span, 159 ft (48.5 m); Length, 155 ft 10 in (47.5 m); Height, 38 ft 8 in (11.78 m);* **Weight:** *Empty, about 160,000 lb (72,600 kg); Loaded, about 340,000 lb (154,000 kg);* **Performance:** *Max speed, 540 mph (870 km/h); Ceiling, about 44,000 ft (13,400 m); Range, 7,800 miles (12,550 km);* **Armament:** *Six 23 mm NS-23 cannon. Bomb load, about 25,000 lb (11,340 kg).*

During the late 1940s, a requirement was put to Soviet aircraft bureaux for a high-speed intercontinental heavy bomber. One of two designs selected was the Tu-95, which was powered by four turboprop engines. The prototype flew in mid-1954 and gave its first display in public at the 1955 Soviet Aviation Day display. The Tu-95 marked a new era in Soviet aircraft

Below *A Tu-20 Bear photographed by an RAF interceptor during exercise 'Northern Merger' in September 1974 (MoD).*

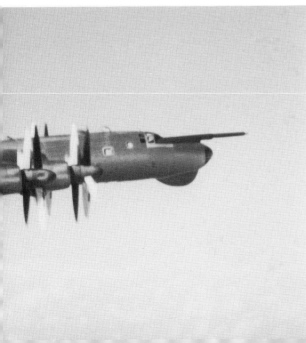

Above *Tupolev Tu-20 Bear viewed from above by a US Navy fighter in May 1971 (US Navy).*

development with all-swept flying surfaces and, in 1956, the year it entered service, led to the development of the Tu-114 airliner.

In about 1961, the Bear first entered service with the Soviet Navy (AV-MF). By the time deliveries of the Tu-20 ceased in about 1962, approximately 300 Bears had been built. The Bear-A is fitted with a chin radar and gun-sight blisters on the rear fuselage. The Bear-B introduced a solid nose in place of the A's glazed frontal area and was equipped for air-to-air refuelling. A centreline attachment was added to carry the AS-3 'Kangaroo' air-to-surface cruise missile. The Bear-C differs little from the B, while the Bear-D has an electronic reconnaissance version radar contained in chin and belly radomes. Later versions are updates of Bear-A models converted for multi-sensor reconnaissance (Bear-E and F). In the mid-1980s, early model Bears were upgraded to Bear-G standard with the 'Kangaroo' missile being replaced by the supersonic AS-4. Production of the Bear has restarted with the Bear-H, armed with the AS-15 subsonic cruise missile.

Around 129 Bears were still serving with the LRA (Long Range Aviation) and Frontal Aviation (similar to the USAF Tactical Air Command) late in 1986. Naval Aviation had approximately 75 Bear-D/E/F/H versions on strength serving in maritime reconnaissance, ASW and ECM roles.

Flight testing of the 'Blackjack' variable geometry strategic bomber was completed in 1986 and the first examples began replacing the Bear-A in 1988.

Above *Soviet Tu-20 Bear photographed from a US Navy interceptor (US Navy).*

VICKERS ARMSTRONG WELLINGTON

Type: *Long-range medium bomber;* **Crew:** *Five-six;* **Manufacturers:** *Vickers-Armstrong, Weybridge, Chester and Blackpool;* **Powerplant:** *(Mk IC) Two Bristol Pegasus XVIII;* **Dimensions:** *Span, 86 ft 2 in (26.26 m); Length, 64 ft 7 in (19.68 m); Height, 17 ft 5 in (5.33 m);* **Weight:** *(Mk IC) Empty, 18,556 lb (8,417 kg); Loaded, 28,500 lb (12,954 kg);* **Performance:** *(Mk IC) Max speed, 235 mph (379 km/h) at 15,500 ft (4,725 m); Range, 1,200 miles (1,932 km); Ceiling, 18,000 ft (5,487 m).*

Mainstay of the RAF heavy night bomber force during the early part of the war and one of the greatest bombers of World War Two, the Vickers Type 271 was a result of Specification B 9/32 of September 1932, which called for an experimental twin-engined day bomber capable of carrying a bomb load of 1,000 lb for

Below *Brace of Merlin-engined Wellington IIs of No 148 Squadron based at Kabrit, Egypt* (IWM).

720 miles (13,218 km) and with a range of 1,500 miles (24,135 km).

R.K. Pierson and his design team applied all that was best in a long line of previous Vickers models. In March 1933, Pierson decided that the new Type 271 should employ a high-wing monoplane design with a fixed undercarriage and should be powered by either two Bristol Mercury VIS2 or the Rolls-Royce Goshawk steam-cooled powerplants. By October, Pierson favoured a retractable undercarriage and with geodetic construction throughout. Geodetics was an ingenious and immensely strong framework which had been devised and developed by Barnes Wallis for the R100 airship.

The Vickers proposal was accepted, and in December 1933 the Air Ministry placed an order for a single prototype Type 271 with Goshawk engines. The Goshawk was later replaced by the air-cooled 850 hp Bristol Pegasus X. The prototype flew for the first time on 15 June 1936, with Captain J. 'Mutt' Summers at the controls. Both front and rear gun turrets were glazed over with Plexiglas and no armament was carried. It proved successful in trials and was exhibited at the annual RAF Display at Hendon. The RAF were particularly impressed with its ability to carry double the bomb load and cover twice the range (3,000 miles/7,827 km) to that originally specified.

In August 1936, the Air Ministry placed an initial production order for 180 of the Vickers type. On 29 January 1937 Specification 29/36 was issued to cover the first production run of 185 Wellington Mk Is. On 19 April, the prototype crashed during diving trials. The fuselage and tail surfaces were revised and the re-design was incorporated in the first production Type 285 Wellington B Mk I, which flew for the first time on 23 December 1937. Subsequent production Wellington Is were fitted with 1,000 hp Pegasus XVIII engines. On 10 October 1938, 99 Squadron became the first in Bomber Command to receive the Wellington B Mk I.

In 1939, production of 189 examples of the Type 408 B Mk IA began. Both Vickers turrets were replaced by Nash and Thompson and each was equipped with two .303 in machine-guns (as was the existing ventral position). Various other improvements were made and the crew complement was increased to six.

The Type 409 B Mk IB did not enter production but the first of some 2,685 Type 415 B Mk IC versions began entering squadron service before the outbreak of war. The B Mk IC was easily distinguishable by the addition of a pair of Vickers K machine-guns installed in each side of the fuselage in place of the earlier ventral position.

On 3 March 1939, the Type 29B Mk II prototype, fitted with 1,145 hp Merlin X engines, flew for the first time and the Type 299 B Mk III prototype, with twin 1,400 hp Bristol Hercules III powerplant, flew for the first time on 16 May 1939. Both types entered production in 1940 as the Type 406 B Mk II and the Type 417 Mk III respectively, and entered service with Bomber Command in 1941. Some 400 Mk II Wellingtons were built and these were followed by 1,519 Mk III models. A Mk IC fitted with a pair of Pratt & Whitney R1830-S3C4-G Twin-Wasps was redesignated Type 410 to become the Mk IV prototype. A total of 220 production models was built.

To increase Wellington production, Vickers established new factories at Chester and at Squires Gate, Blackpool. Wellingtons were being produced at the rate of 134 a month in September 1940 and by the spring of 1941 this had grown to more than double this figure.

Late in 1939 Vickers produced two high-altitude prototypes in response to Air Ministry specification B.23/39, which called for the development of a high-altitude conversion of the Wellington. The specification stipulated that the type had to be capable of attaining an altitude of 40,000 ft (12,195 m), i.e., to put it

Wellington IC P9249 HD-T of 38 Squadron. On 16 June 1940 it crashed on approach to RAF Marham, killing its pilot and seriously injuring two of its crew (Vickers).

out of reach of enemy flak and fighters. Both prototypes had a special cigar shaped fuselage with a pressurized cabin in the nose to simulate conditions at 10,000 ft (3,049 m). Originally, it was planned to fit two 1,650 hp Bristol Hercules VIII engines but production difficulties dictated the use of the Hercules III powerplant.

The first of the two Mk V prototypes (R3298), made its maiden flight in September 1940 and achieved a height of 30,000 ft (9,146 m). Only one Mk V model (the second off the production lines) was completed and 19 more were finished to Mk VI standard. Meanwhile, the first production aircraft was redesignated the Mk VI prototype and, as such, fitted with two 1,600 hp Rolls-Royce Merlin 60 RM6SM engines. In April 1941, this engine was bench tested with a two-stage supercharger. Without such a device, the Wellington had no chance of reaching the prescribed 40,000 ft (12,195 m).

On 19 August 1941 a further 100 Mk VIs were ordered, although 56 were later cancelled. The majority of the survivors became Mk VIs equipped with Gee navigational systems. Late in March 1942, 109 Squadron at Tempsford received four Wellington Mk VIs for commencement of trials with the Oboe radar blind bombing device. A week before it was almost decided to use the Mk VI operationally, it was rejected in favour of the Mosquito. The Mk VI had proved too slow and had other disadvantages which made it unsuitable for use in the Oboe squadrons.

In the spring of 1942 the first Wellington GR Mk VIIIs entered service with Coastal Command. Altogether, some 394 GR Mk VIIIs were built. As on the Mk IC, the type was fitted with the Bristol Pegasus XVIII powerplant. The GR Mk VIII differed from the Mk IC in being the first to be equipped with ASV Mk II radar and fitted with radar masts on top of the fuselage. Some versions also carried Leigh Lights.

The GR Mk VIII was followed by a series of more advanced marks of Wellington. Some 180 Mk XIs were built at Squires Gate and were

followed by 843 Mk XIII models. Meanwhile, 58 Mk XII versions were produced at Chester and Weybridge, and Squires Gate and Chester turned out a further 841 Mk XIVs. Altogether some 3,406 Wellingtons were built at Blackpool, with the last leaving the production lines on 13 October 1945.

Both the XI and XII versions were powered by Hercules VI or XVI powerplants and carried no nose turret or radar masts on top of the fuselage. An ASV Mk III radar was housed in a chin radome beneath the nose. Beneath the wing, provision was made for two 18 in torpedoes and a retractable Leigh Light was installed in the bomb bay. ASV II radar and masts and the nose turret were reintroduced on the Mk XIII which was fitted with two Bristol Hercules XVII engines. The final general reconnaissance version, the Mk XIV, differed little from the Mk XII but was powered by Hercules XVII engines.

As early as December 1941, Wellington Mk ICs were converted for mine laying and torpedo bombing operations in the Mediterranean. Wellingtons flew anti-submarine operations in Europe and the Far East until the end of the war. Two Wellington bomber squadrons—99 and 215—also served in the Far East.

The Wellington X, which entered service

with RAF Bomber Command in 1943, was the final bomber version to see service in World War Two. An improved version of the B Mk III, it was powered by two Bristol Hercules XVI engines and some 3,804 examples were built. At one stage the Wellington X equipped some 25 OTUs (Operational Training Units) and it saw widespread service in the Middle East.

With the end of the war in Europe, the Wellington almost completely disappeared from the RAF inventory, although several Wellington Xs were revamped by Boulton Paul for extended service as crew trainers with Flying Training Command. Altogether, some 11,461 Wellingtons of all marks were built.

VICKERS VIMY-VIRGINIA

Type: *Heavy night bomber*; **Crew:** *Four*; **Manufacturers:** *Vickers Aviation, Weybridge, Surrey*; **Powerplant:** *(Virginia X) Two Napier Lion V*; **Dimensions:** *Span, 87 ft 8 in (26.7 m); Length, 62 ft 2¾ in (18.9 m); Height, 18 ft 2 in (5.5 m);* **Weight:** *Empty, 9,650 lb (4,386 kg); Loaded, 17,600 lb (8,000 kg);* **Performance:** *Max speed, 108 mph (174 km/h) at 4,920 ft (1,500 m); Range, 985 miles (1,586 km); Ceiling, 15,530 ft (4,734 m);* **Armament:** *Three Lewis guns. Bomb load, 3,000 lb (1,363 kg).*

After the First World War, Britain persisted with slow and cumbersome biplane bombers without any significant increase in performance. Among the first of these was the Vickers Vimy, which flew for the first time on 30 November 1917. The type was just too late to see action, equipping No 58 Squadron in Egypt in July 1919 and D Flight of No 100 Squadron at Spittlegate, Yorkshire.

The most famous Vickers Vimy is undoubtedly the one used by Captain John Alcock and Lieutenant Arthur Whitten Brown in the first non-stop transatlantic flight, from St John's, Newfoundland to Clifden, County Galway, on 14/15 June 1919. This Vimy was a modified version, stripped of all its military equipment and carried 865 imperial gallons of fuel instead of the normal 516 gallons. It completed the 1,890 mile (3,043 km) journey in 16 hours 27 minutes. Both airmen were later knighted and the Vimy is today on display at the Science Museum in London.

The Vimy subsequently equipped Nos 45, 70 and 216 Squadrons in Egypt, but at home No 100 Squadron remained the only twin-engined

Vickers Virginia J6856 prototype with Napier Lion engines pictured at Brooklands before the first flight on 22 November 1922 (Vickers).

Above *Rolls-Royce Eagle VIII engined Vickers Vimy IV F8618 of No 70 Squadron, RAF, in Egypt in the 1920s* (Norfolk & Suffolk Aviation Museum).

bomber unit in service until the formation of No 7 Squadron at Bircham Newton, Norfolk in June 1923. Post-war re-armament was alarmingly slow and it was not until April 1924 that Nos 9 and 58 Squadrons joined the home-based bomber force.

The Vimy was replaced in first-line service by the Vickers Virginia in 1924/25, but remained operational with No 502 Squadron in Northern Ireland until as late as 1929. In the twilight of its career the Vimy was used in various training roles until 1931.

VICKERS VALIANT

Type: *Strategic bomber*; **Crew:** *Five*; **Manufacturers:** *Vickers-Armstrong, Weybridge, Surrey*; **Powerplant:** *Four Rolls-Royce Avon 201 Turbojets*; **Dimensions:** *Span, 114 ft 4 in (34.8 m); Length, 108 ft 3 in (33 m); Height, 32 ft 2 in (9.81 m);* **Weight:** *Empty, 75,881 lb (34,491 kg); Loaded, 140,000 lb (63,636 kg);* **Performance:** *Max speed, 567 mph (913 km/h) at 30,000 ft (9,146 m); Range, 4.500 miles (7,246 km); Ceiling, 54,000 ft (16,463 m);* **Armament:** *None. Conventional or nuclear bomb load, 21,000 lb (9,545 kg).*

The Valiant was the first of the 'V' Class four-jet bombers to enter RAF service, replacing the Canberras and Lincolns of 3 Group Bomber Command in 1955. The prototype made its maiden flight on 18 May 1951, but was destroyed during a test flight over Hampshire on 12 January 1952. A second was built and flew for the first time on 11 April 1952. The first of five pre-production aircraft flew at Brooklands on 22 December 1953. The first Valiant B I entered RAF service on 8 February 1955 with No 138 Squadron at Gaydon.

Valiants were followed into service by 11 long-range strategic reconnaissance versions, the B (PR) I and 14 B (PR) K Mk Is and 45 BK Mk IIs. Both the latter marks were capable of operating as a bomber or as a flight refuelling

tanker. In October-November 1956, Valiants of Nos 138, 148, 207 and 214 Squadrons based at Luqa, Malta, took part in conventional bombing operations over Egypt during the Anglo-French intervention in the Suez Canal Zone. On 31 October, V-bombers were first used operationally when Valiants bombed Almaza airfield.

On 11 October 1956, a Valiant of No 49 Squadron carried the first British operational atomic bomb to be dropped from an aircraft, at Maralinga, Australia. On 15 May 1957, a Valiant of the same Squadron dropped the first British Hydrogen bomb during Operation 'Grapple' on Christmas Island in the Pacific.

Vickers Valiant BK Mk I WZ365 in flight (Vickers).

Successful air-to-air refuelling trials were carried out using Valiant tanker and receiver aircraft from No 214 Squadron in February 1958. On 9 July 1959 a Valiant from this Squadron made the first non-stop flight from the UK to Cape Town covering a distance of 6,060 miles (9,758 km) after being twice refuelled in the air. In May 1960 a Valiant, again from No 214 Squadron, made a non-stop flight from the United Kingdom to Singapore after twice being refuelled in the air by Valiant tankers operating

Vickers Valiant BK Mk I XD823 with nose probe for in-flight refuelling (Vickers).

from Cyprus and from Pakistan.

In 1964 Valiants were switched to the low-level role, but in August that year serious metal fatigue was discovered in the airframes and the following January all Valiants were withdrawn from service and subsequently scrapped. Some 104 aircraft had been built and had equipped ten squadrons in Bomber Command.

INDEX

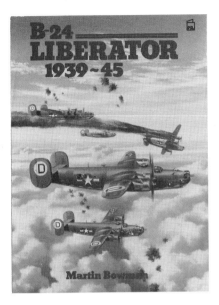

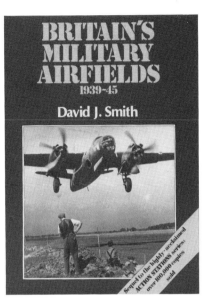

During the Second World War, the Liberator bomber was produced in far greater quantities than any other American aircraft and served with fifteen air forces in a variety of roles.

The B-24 is perhaps best remembered for its daylight raids with the United States 8th and 15th Air Forces and its mission to Ploesti in August 1943, but these were just a small part of the work of this amazing aircraft. It provided invaluable support to the US Navy in the Pacific, with its formidable low-level bombing of Japanese targets, and was even involved with the RAF, flying thousands of miles with the South East Asia Command in India and Burma, as well as making a significant contribution to the Battle of the Atlantic.

This fascinating book also covers the Liberator's less well-known exploits. It had a chequered career as a VIP and troop carrier, and it was used for dropping spies and as an airborne fuel tanker.

Of the 18,888 Liberators built during the Second World War, only eight are known to exist today, but the B-24 is assured of a place in history as the most versatile aircraft of the war, and is fondly recalled by those who knew the aircraft, and anyone with an interest in aviation and wartime history.

Few people live more than 10 miles away from at least one abandoned airfield, and while to some they are an eyesore, to many others they are a fascinating piece of Britain's heritage, and there is an increasing awareness of their historical importance.

Published to complement PSL's best-selling *Action Stations* series, this book also stands on its own as a detailed look at the development of military airfields in Britain from the days before the First World War to 1945, when their numbers reached an all-time high.

The largest airfield construction programme of our history peaked in 1942, resulting in Britain being referred to as a vast aircraft carrier anchored off the north-west coast of Europe. By the end of the war, some 360,000 acres of land were occupied by airfields, including 160 million square yards of concrete.

As well as strategic requirements, site selection, planning and construction, the book also covers the story of the paved runaway debate, Royal Naval Air Stations, flying boat bases, Satellite Landing Grounds and support functions such as bombing and firing ranges, buildings, camouflage, lighting and navigation aids. There is also a comprehensive list of airfield memorials.

The WORLD ENCYCLOPAEDIA OF MODERN AIR WEAPONS is a detailed, comprehensive reference guide to the weapons available to the air arms of today's military forces. Every air-to-air, anti-tank, anti-ship and submarine, anti-personnel or other air-to-surface bomb, rocket or missile is described and (where possible) illustrated, as is every significant aircraft-mounted gun or cannon currently in service. The result is an essential information source for anyone professionally involved in the industry or keenly interested in aviation. No other comparable detailed reference source to today's aerial weaponry exists in one volume, even within normally classified literature.

The earlier companion volume, the WORLD ENCYCLOPAEDIA OF MODERN AIRCRAFT ARMAMENT, puts the other side of the weaponry/armament equation: it gives full details of the weapons and arms carrying capabilities of every significant combat aircraft currently in service with the air arms of NATO, the Soviet Union and the Warsaw Pact as well as the non-aligned nations and the People's Republic of China. Each aircraft is described, as seen by battlefield planners, in terms of the weapons options available to it and the electronics/avionics support that it can offer in self-defence or to ensure accurate delivery of the stores carried. Alongside their fixed-wing counterparts are to be found explanations of the weapon systems of all current front-line helicopter types in service, reflecting an increasingly significant and potent development on the modern battlefield.

The mass of information in these two books – on weapons and the abilities of aircraft to carry them – has been meticulously gathered at first hand, much of it direct from the weapons and aircraft manufacturers themselves. Together they form an indispensable reference to modern aerial warfare.